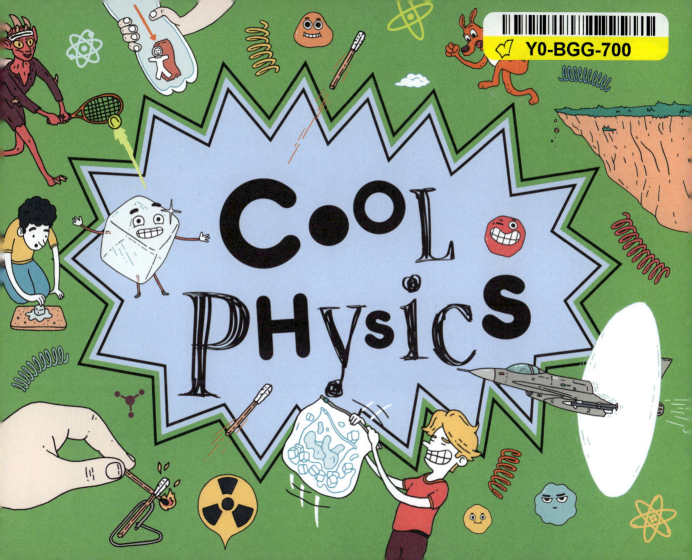

CoOL PHysiCS

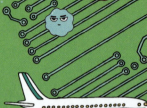

First published in Great Britain 2017 by Pavilion Children's Books
This edition published in Great Britain 2024 by Dean, part of Farshore
An imprint of HarperCollins*Publishers*
1 London Bridge Street, London SE1 9GF
www.farshore.co.uk

HarperCollins*Publishers*
Macken House, 39/40 Mayor Street Upper
Dublin 1, D01 C9W8

ISBN 978 0 00 873677 4
Printed in China
001

A CIP catalogue record for this book is available from the British Library.

MIX
Paper | Supporting
responsible forestry
FSC™ C007454
FSC
www.fsc.org

This book contains FSC™ certified paper and other controlled
sources to ensure responsible forest management.

For more information visit: www.harpercollins.co.uk/green

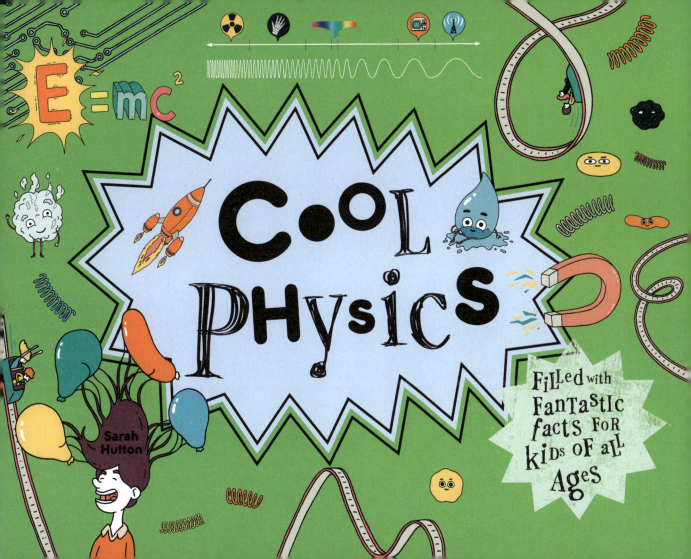

$E = mc^2$

Cool Physics

Sarah Hutton

Filled with Fantastic facts For kids OF aLL Ages

Contents

Welcome to *Cool Physics*

When I was young I loved taking things apart in an effort to understand how they worked. My parents very quickly learnt that I had an intuitive ability to use a screwdriver, and so made sure I was never left alone with electronics, or left anything plugged in when it wasn't in use. Over time I even learnt how to put things back together again! As I got older I gave up taking electronics apart to understand them and began studying physics as a way of getting answers to my questions.

Physics is the key to understanding the world around us, the world inside us, and the world beyond us. It is the most basic and fundamental science. It includes the study of the Universe from the largest galaxies to the smallest subatomic particles.

Physics can challenge our imagination with concepts like relativity and grand unified theories, and it leads to great discoveries, like computers and lasers, that in turn lead to technologies that change our lives – from healing joints to curing cancer to developing sustainable energy solutions.

Today, I still love learning about physics, but I spend most of my time helping others understand more about the subject through lectures, workshops and even this book. Over the following pages you can learn about famous physicists, particle physics, astronomy and thermodynamics. It won't teach everything there is to know about physics – I'd need thousands of books to be able to do that! But hopefully it will encourage you to find out more about the subject, and maybe to even go on to discover new theories about how the world around us works.

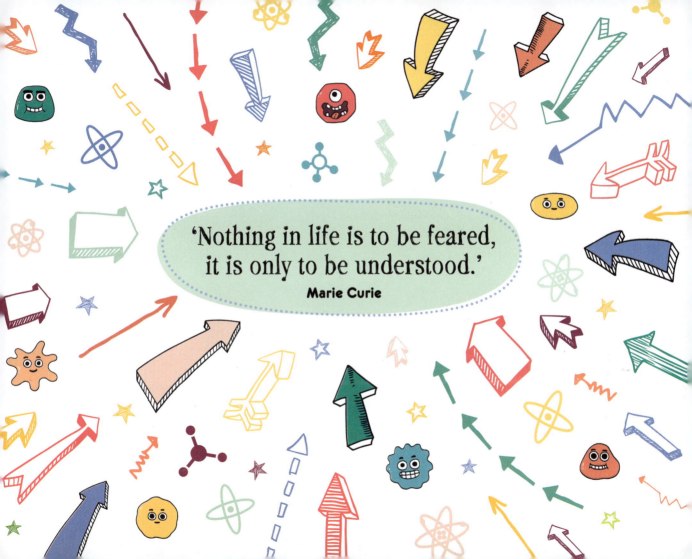

'Nothing in life is to be feared,
it is only to be understood.'

Marie Curie

Physics Timeline

Discoveries in physics have been happening for thousands of years, even before physics became a subject in its own right – it used to be classed as part of the physical sciences along with chemistry and maths. Here are some important milestones on physics' journey of self-discovery, and the achievements that have helped turn the field into what we recognise today.

Third century BC Aristarchus proposes a sun-centred model of the Solar System

150BC Seleucus of Seleucia discovers that the Moon causes tides

150AD Ptolemy proposes an earth-centred model of the Solar System

1054 Chinese and Native American astronomers observe the Crab supernova explosion

1100 A lodestone is first used as a compass

1572 Tycho Brahe observes the supernova in Cassiopeia

1613 Galileo Galilei uses sunspots to demonstrate the rotation of the Sun

1619 Johannes Kepler finishes his three laws of planetary motion

1665 Isaac Newton invents his calculus

1678 Christiaan Huygens states his principle of wavefront sources

1752 Benjamin Franklin shows that lightning is electricity

1783 John Michell first theorises about black holes

1798 Henry Cavendish measures the gravitational constant and determines the mass of the Earth

1801 Thomas Young demonstrates the wave nature of light and the principle of interference

1821 Michael Faraday builds an electric motor

1827 Robert Brown discovers Brownian motion

1831 Faraday discovers electromagnetic induction

1848 Lord Kelvin discovers the absolute zero point of temperature

1850 Fizeau and Foucault measure the speed of light in water and find that it is slower than in air, supporting the wave model of light

1897 J.J. Thomson discovers the electron

1898 Marie Curie coins the term 'radioactivity'

1905 Albert Einstein completes his theory of special relativity

1911 Ernest Rutherford discovers the shape of the atomic nucleus

1913 Niels Bohr presents the first quantum model of the atom

1915 Albert Einstein completes his theory of general relativity

1927 Werner Heisenberg states the quantum uncertainty principle

1965 Arno Penzias and Robert Wilson discover the cosmic microwave background radiation

1967 Jocelyn Bell Burnell discovers the first pulsar

1998 Scientists find the expansion of the universe is accelerating

2012 Higgs boson discovered at CERN

2016 Gravitational waves from a black hole merger are discovered by the LIGO team

Eureka!

There was once a fellow named Archimedes, born in around 287bc in the city of Syracuse in Sicily. He was a mathematician, inventor, engineer, philosopher and astronomer.

The king's problem solver

One day Archimedes was summoned by the King of Sicily to investigate whether a goldsmith had cheated him. The king had given the goldsmith the exact amount of gold needed to make a crown. However, when the crown was complete, the king suspected that the goldsmith had cheated and slipped some silver into the crown, keeping some of the gold for himself. The king asked Archimedes to find out, but there was a catch – he couldn't do any damage to the crown.

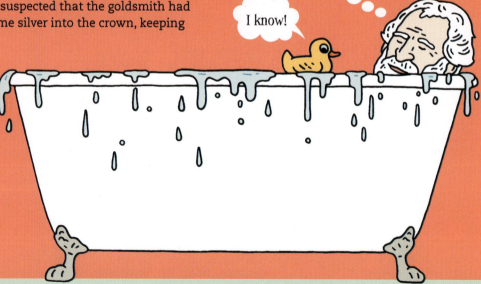

Now, how am I going to solve this?

I know!

Density

Archimedes needed to check the crown's density to see if it matched the density of gold. Density is the measure of an object's mass divided by its volume. Gold is more dense than silver, so if there was silver in the crown, its density would be less than if it was pure gold. All Archimedes needed to do was measure the mass of the crown and then measure its volume to work out its density. However, that was where the problem lay; measuring the volume of the crown wasn't easy. It wasn't a regular shape like a ball or a cube and so had no easy sides to measure.

Archimedes was puzzled by this problem until one day, while taking a bath, he noticed that the water level rose and overflowed as he lowered himself into the tub. The more he sank into the tub, the more water poured out, and he realised that the amount of water escaping was equal to the amount of his body submerged in the tub. According to legend, this discovery excited him so much that he jumped out of the tub and ran naked through the streets shouting 'Eureka!'

He had found a way to solve the king's problem – give the crown a bath! By placing it in water and seeing how much water was displaced, he could measure the volume and calculate the density of the crown. When Archimedes went back to the king and did his test, he found that the goldsmith had indeed cheated the king!

Get Physical!

Using the way an object displaces water to measure its volume is now called the Archimedes Principle. The next time you take a bath you can see the Archimedes Principle in action; who knows, maybe you'll have a genius idea of your own!

EUREKA!

Fitting the World in a Matchbox

Suppose you tried to build the world we live in. Where would you start?

You'd need to be able to build people . . . houses . . . mountains . . . and millions of other things. But you could make things easier for yourself, just by having several different types of atoms. With these you could build everything you want and more. Atoms are the tiny building blocks from which everything around us is constructed.

What is an atom?

Take anything apart and you'll find something smaller inside. There are engines inside planes and cars, pips inside fruit, brains inside people, and stuffing inside teddy bears. Keep going and eventually you'll find that all the stuff around us is made from different types of atoms.

Living things, for example, are mostly made from the atoms carbon, hydrogen and oxygen. These are just three of over a hundred chemical elements that scientists have discovered. You can make virtually anything you can think of by joining atoms of different elements together like tiny Lego blocks.

An atom is the smallest possible amount of a chemical element – so an atom of gold is the smallest amount of gold you can possibly have. And it really is small: a single atom is about 100,000 times thinner than a human hair.

Get Physical!

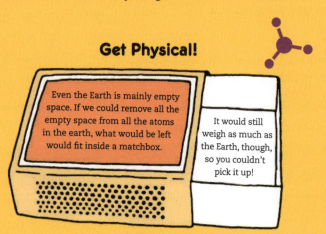

Even the Earth is mainly empty space. If we could remove all the empty space from all the atoms in the earth, what would be left would fit inside a matchbox.

It would still weigh as much as the Earth, though, so you couldn't pick it up!

Modelling an atom

In ancient times, people thought atoms were the smallest possible things in the world. In fact, the word atom comes from a Greek word, *atomos*, meaning indivisible. Today, we know this isn't true, and we know that we can break atoms down into smaller pieces called subatomic particles. These particles are called protons, neutrons and electrons.

The simplest model of the atom has the protons and neutrons packed together tightly in a nucleus in the middle surrounded by shells of electrons. While this image is quite good at explaining how atoms work and interact with each other, it does not explain how big the different parts of the atom are in relation to each other.

Imagine instead that every atom is the size of a large football stadium. The nucleus would be the size of a cricket ball in the centre spot and the electrons would be tiny flies whizzing around the stands. There is nothing else. Most of the atom is just empty space. Most of you – and everything around you – is just empty space.

The Densest Place in the Universe

You have already seen that atoms are actually mainly empty space, and that if we remove this then we could fit the Earth into a matchbox. What would happen if we could do the same thing to a star?

A stellar phoenix

When stars between four and eight times the mass of the Sun explode in a violent supernova, their outer layers can blow off in a spectacular display, leaving behind a small, dense core that continues to collapse. Gravity presses the material in on itself so tightly that protons and electrons combine to make neutrons, hence the term 'neutron star'.

This turns a star with a diameter of 1 billion km into an extremely dense sphere with a diameter of just 20km! Squishing a star down so much creates some very strange results. For example, gravity is around a billion times stronger on a neutron star, causing an effect called gravitational lensing, where the star is so dense it distorts space and acts like a giant magnifying glass, bending light rays as they pass by it. The power released as the star collapses causes the star to start spinning, starting fast and getting slower over time. The slowest (and oldest) neutron stars spin around once per second but the fastest ones known spin around 700 times per second!

If a neutron star is part of a binary system (where two stars orbit each other) and the other star survives the deadly blast from its supernova, things can get even more interesting. If the second star is less massive than our Sun, the neutron star pulls mass from its companion into a 'Roche lobe', a balloon-like cloud of material that orbits the neutron star. Companion stars up to 10 times the Sun's mass create similar mass transfers that are more unstable and don't last as long. Stars more than 10 times as massive as the Sun transfer material in the form of stellar wind. The material flows along the magnetic poles of the neutron star, creating X-ray pulsations as it is heated.

Woo-hoo!

Get Physical!

One of the most well-known types of neutron star is a pulsar. A pulsar is a neutron star that has jets of materials streaming out at nearly the speed of light. As these beams move past Earth, they flash like the bulb of a lighthouse – imagine a child with a torch whirling round on a swivel chair!

Famous Physicists 1

Ouch!

Sir Isaac Newton (1643–1727)

Sir Isaac Newton is mentioned throughout this book for his pioneering work on gravity, motion and optics, as well as his revolutionary work in maths, but his family never wanted him to go into academia. They wanted him to be a farmer, and even when he went to university, he initially studied law. While Newton made many remarkable discoveries he did not take criticism well, and he often used his position as president of the Royal Society to bury the work of those who had different theories to him.

Albert Einstein (1879–1955)

Albert Einstein was a German physicist who revolutionised physics with his theories of relativity and the equation $E=mc^2$. While he was very good at maths and science at school, he didn't like school and preferred to learn on his own. Even though his theories of relativity are his most famous discovery, Einstein was actually awarded the Nobel Prize in Physics for his explanation of the photoelectric effect.

As a Jew, he was forced to leave Germany after he became a target for the Nazi Party. He moved to the US and became an American citizen in 1940. Einstein is generally considered the most influential physicist of the twentieth century. He was even named as 'Person of the Century' by TIME magazine in 1999.

> I ... a universe of atoms, an atom in the Universe.

Sir Isaac Newton was also warden of the Royal Mint and took very seriously his role in reforming the currency and getting rid of corruption.

Get Physical!

Richard Feynman (1918–88)

Richard Feynman was an American theoretical physicist who not only developed a completely new way of thinking about particle physics, but was also a brilliant teacher who won many teaching prizes. He also loved playing the bongo drums!

During his PhD Feynman would often attend advanced lectures on biological sciences, as he enjoyed them and didn't think that just because he studied physics he shouldn't be allowed to learn about other subjects as well. Throughout his academic career Feynman enjoyed teaching students, and he published many books that evolved out of his lecture courses.

During the Second World War Feynman was involved in the development of the atomic bomb as part of the Manhattan Project. He was head of the theoretical division and was also tasked with safety at the testing site.

> If I had only known, I would have been a locksmith.

Chaos from Order

When scientists originally studied thermodynamics, they were really studying heat or, in other words, thermal energy. Heat can do anything: move from one area to another, get atoms excited, and even increase energy. When you increase the heat in a system, you are really increasing the amount of energy in the system. Now you know that, you can see that the study of thermodynamics is actually the study of energy moving in and out of systems, so it's not as scary as it sounds!

Hot atoms

All of this energy is moving around the world, but you need to remember that it all happens on a really small scale. It's the atoms and molecules that are transmitting these tiny amounts of energy. When heat moves from one area to another, it's because millions of atoms and molecules are all working together. Those millions of pieces become the energy flow throughout the entire planet.

Heat will move from one place to another if there is a difference in temperature between the two. If you have two identical places with equal temperatures, there will be no flow of energy. When you have two areas with different temperatures, the energy will start to flow. Areas of high temperature give off energy to areas with lower temperature. There is a constant flow of energy throughout the Universe. Heat is only one type of that energy.

Increasing energy, increasing entropy

Another big idea in thermodynamics is the concept of energy changing the freedom of molecules. For example, when you change the state of a system (solid, liquid, gas), the atoms and molecules have different arrangements and degrees of freedom to move. That increase in freedom (also called randomness or disorder) is called entropy.

Atoms are able to move around more and there is more activity. Places will, over time, increase their entropy according to the laws of thermodynamics, which means that everything (on the microscope scale) is becoming more random and chaotic over time, no matter how ordered things were to start with.

This means that the next time you're asked to tidy your room you can just say you are creating a large-scale demonstration of entropy!

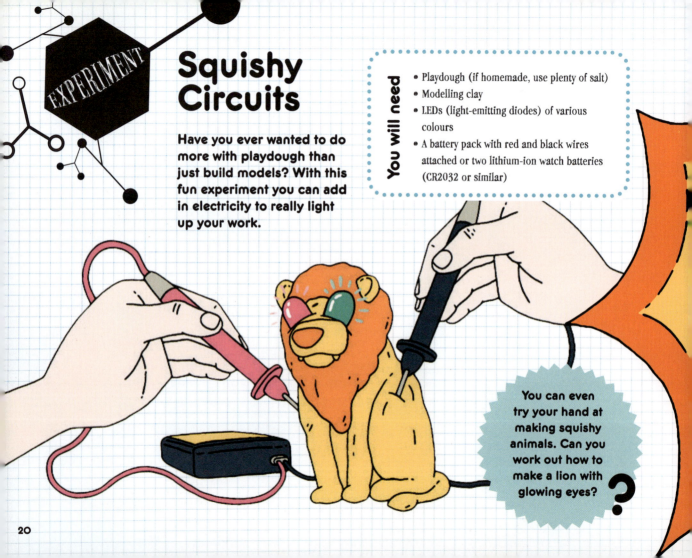

Squishy Circuits

Have you ever wanted to do more with playdough than just build models? With this fun experiment you can add in electricity to really light up your work.

You will need

- Playdough (if homemade, use plenty of salt)
- Modelling clay
- LEDs (light-emitting diodes) of various colours
- A battery pack with red and black wires attached or two lithium-ion watch batteries (CR2032 or similar)

You can even try your hand at making squishy animals. Can you work out how to make a lion with glowing eyes?

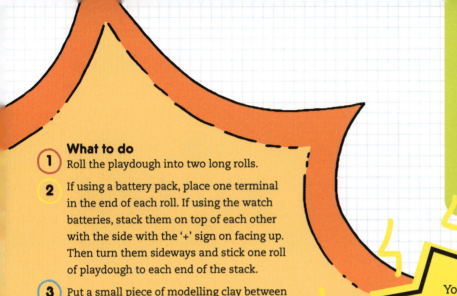

What to do

1. Roll the playdough into two long rolls.

2. If using a battery pack, place one terminal in the end of each roll. If using the watch batteries, stack them on top of each other with the side with the '+' sign on facing up. Then turn them sideways and stick one roll of playdough to each end of the stack.

3. Put a small piece of modelling clay between the open ends of the playdough to form a complete loop.

4. Place an LED over the modelling clay, making sure that the metal ends of the LED are securely in the playdough. Make sure the long end of the LED joins up to the red terminal of the battery pack or the '+' side of the watch battery stack.

How it works
The salts in the playdough make it conductive, allowing electricity to flow through it. The modelling clay is not conductive so it acts as a barrier and forces the electricity to flow through the LEDs.

You have now made your first squishy circuit! You have made a series circuit where everything is in a single loop and the electricity can only flow one way around the circuit. The other type of circuit is called a parallel circuit, where the electricity can split up and go through different branches. You can now build different circuits and see how many LEDs you can make light up.

Maxwell's Demon

In 1871, the Scottish physicist James Clerk Maxwell proposed a thought experiment.

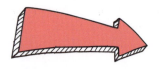

A wall separates two compartments filled with gas. A little demon sits by an opening in the wall, holding a bat. The demon looks at oncoming gas molecules and, depending on their speeds, either allows them through the opening or knocks them away. The object of the game is to eventually collect all the molecules faster than average on one side, and the slower ones on the other side.

This means that the demon ends up with a hot, high-pressure gas on one side, and a cold, low-pressure gas on the other. Even though the conservation of energy principle is not violated, as there is the same amount of energy in the overall container at the beginning and the end, we have managed to rearrange the heat in the system. If we wanted to we could now take energy out of the system – for example, we could use the hot gas to drive an engine.

Doing the impossible

In Maxwell's thought experiment the demon manages to *decrease* the entropy of the system. In other words, it increases the amount of energy available by increasing its knowledge about the motion of all the molecules.

Thermodynamics says this is impossible, you can only ever increase entropy or, more precisely, you can decrease it in one place as long as that is balanced by at least as big an increase somewhere else.

Get Physical!

Real-life versions of Maxwellian demons actually occur in living systems, such as the ion channels and pumps that make our nervous systems work, including our minds. These molecular-sized mechanisms are no longer found only in biology, however: they're also the subject of the emerging field of nanotechnology.

So can it work?

Well, any real 'demon' that does this would not be a disembodied spirit receiving its information telepathically. To acquire information about the world you must physically interact with it. In determining what side of the gate a molecule must be on, the demon must store information about the state of the molecule. Eventually, the demon will run out of information storage space and must begin to erase the information that has been previously gathered. Erasing information is a thermodynamically irreversible process that increases the entropy of a system. Maxwell's demon therefore reveals a deep connection between thermodynamics and information theory, which is still being researched today.

What Goes Up Must Come Down

Gravity is something that everybody is familiar with: the force that keeps everything stuck to the Earth. But what is it? Gravity, or to give it its more scientific name, the *force of gravitational attraction*, is a force that is felt by any object with mass when it is near another object with mass. The more massive an object is, the greater the force. This is why you are attracted towards the Earth, but not to somebody walking down the street. Distance also matters, and the closer you are to an object, the stronger the force is.

Making the world go round

Gravity is incredibly important to our everyday lives. Without Earth's gravity we would fly right off it as it spins round. Gravity is also the most important force in space. It's the gravitational force between the Sun and the Earth that keeps the Earth in orbit around the Sun. It's the force that causes galaxies to form and merge. It's also the force responsible for the formation of the first atoms, molecules and stars after the Big Bang.

Who discovered gravity?

The first person who dropped something heavy on their toe knew something was going on, but gravity was first mathematically described by Sir Isaac Newton. His theory is called *Newton's law of universal gravitation* and explains the relationship between mass, distance and the resultant force. Later, Albert Einstein would update this theory in his theory of relativity, describing how gravity affects the quantum world.

Get Physical!

The tides on Earth are caused by the gravitational attraction between the Moon and the Earth. The water in the sea is attracted to the Moon, making it bulge in that direction. The bulge then follows the Moon as the Earth turns beneath it.

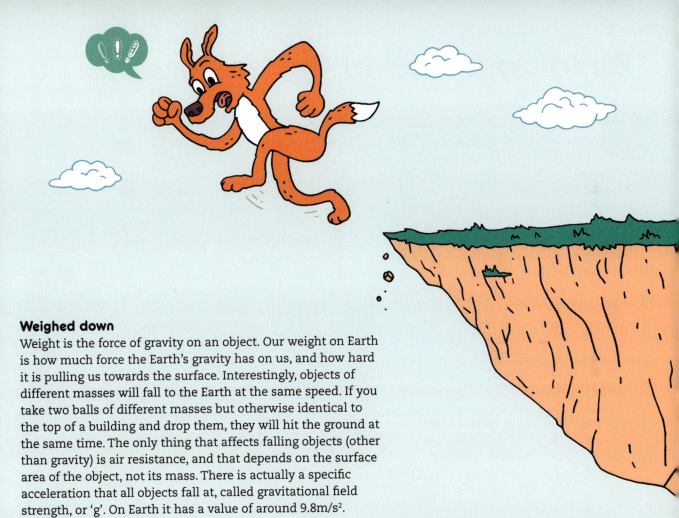

Weighed down

Weight is the force of gravity on an object. Our weight on Earth is how much force the Earth's gravity has on us, and how hard it is pulling us towards the surface. Interestingly, objects of different masses will fall to the Earth at the same speed. If you take two balls of different masses but otherwise identical to the top of a building and drop them, they will hit the ground at the same time. The only thing that affects falling objects (other than gravity) is air resistance, and that depends on the surface area of the object, not its mass. There is actually a specific acceleration that all objects fall at, called gravitational field strength, or 'g'. On Earth it has a value of around $9.8m/s^2$.

Building Blocks of the Universe

Have you ever taken something apart to find out what it was made of? In many cases this just results in broken electronics or stuffing all over the room, but this is one of the ways physicists work out what the Universe is made of.

Smaller than small

In 1968, scientists working on the SLAC (Stanford Linear Accelerator Center) experiment in California smashed electrons into protons and neutrons. They found that the electrons didn't behave as expected, which could only be explained if the protons and neutrons were made up of smaller particles. These particles, named quarks after a line in James Joyce's novel *Finnegans Wake*, had been theorised in 1964.

Strange flavours

Quarks are always found in combinations, and cannot, so far as is known, occur by themselves. So far, six different types, called flavours, have been found: *up, down, strange, charmed, top* and *bottom*. The existence of the top quark, the last of the six to be confirmed, was verified in 1995. These quarks can combine in many different ways to form more than 100 different types of particles.

The particular combinations of quarks determine the type of particles formed. A proton, for instance, is composed of two up quarks and a down quark, while a neutron is composed of one up and two downs. It is believed that all of the matter in the Universe is made up of quarks and leptons. See page 30 for more about leptons.

Bags of particles

Any particle made of quarks is called a hadron. In particular, a hadron made up of three quarks – such as a proton or neutron – is called a baryon, while a particle made up of two quarks (strictly speaking, a quark and an antiquark) is called a meson.

While much has been learned about the properties of quarks, less is known about how they are arranged inside hadrons. One commonly used illustration is called the *bag model*, where the hadron is like a tiny bag containing the quarks. Inside the bag the quarks can go wherever they please, but the so-called strong force prevents them from straying too far from each other and leaving the bag.

Is there anything else?

Quarks can jump from bag to bag in nuclear reactions, changing from one kind of hadron to another, but they can never exist outside a bag that has at least one other quark inside. If it is true that a bag can never be emptied and a single quark studied, we may never know if quarks are really fundamental particles. Some scientists suspect that quarks and leptons may be made of yet smaller pieces.

But do the known quarks and leptons answer the question 'What is the Universe made of?' Or are they yet another starting point?

Indoor Clouds

While clouds outside may mean rain is on the way (if it's not already raining), indoor clouds can make even the dullest day exciting!

- Pint glass
- Small bowl
- Hot water
- Ice
- Aerosol spray (e.g. deodorant)

What to do

1 Pour 5cm of hot water into the pint glass.

2 Swirl the water around the glass to warm it up.

3 Place the ice cubes in the small bowl.

4 Balance the bowl on top of the pint glass.

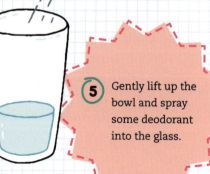

5 Gently lift up the bowl and spray some deodorant into the glass.

How it works

Clouds form when warm, moist air cools and the water condenses into droplets. But the droplets need a surface on which to form. In the Earth's atmosphere this surface is provided by dust particles. In our experiment it's particles from the aerosol. If we didn't use the aerosol, the water would just condense on the bottom of the bowl and drop down once enough water had collected.

In places of drought scientists are trying to modify the weather and create artificial clouds by spreading small particles in the air that water can condense onto. This process is known as cloud seeding.

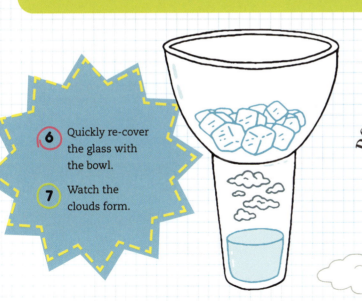

6 Quickly re-cover the glass with the bowl.

7 Watch the clouds form.

DO TRY THIS AT HOME!

Check to see if you can create clouds without using the aerosol. Is there an optimum amount of spray to use? Does changing the temperature of the hot water or the amount of ice make any difference?

The Standard Model

The work of thousands of physicists since the 1930s has resulted in a remarkable insight into the structure of matter: everything in the Universe is made from a few basic building blocks called fundamental particles, governed by four fundamental forces.

Our best understanding of how these particles and three of these forces are related to each other is encapsulated in the 'Standard Model' of particle physics. Over time and through many experiments, the Standard Model has become a well-established theory in physics.

Matter matters

All matter around us is made of elementary, or fundamental, particles, the building blocks of matter. These particles occur in two basic types called quarks and leptons. Each group consists of six particles, which are related in pairs, or 'generations'.

The lightest and most stable particles make up the first generation, while the heavier and less stable particles belong to the second and third generations. All stable matter in the Universe is made from particles that belong to the first generation; any heavier particles quickly decay to the next most stable level. Like the quarks explained on page 26, the six leptons are also arranged in three generations:

1 The **electron** and the **electron neutrino**

2 The **muon** and the **muon neutrino**

3 The **tau** and the **tau neutrino**

The electron, the muon and the tau all have an electric charge and a sizeable mass, whereas the neutrinos are electrically neutral and have very little mass.

Carrying the force

There are four fundamental forces at work in the Universe, which you'll learn about on page 104. All the forces have different strengths and work over different ranges. Three of them result from the exchange of force-carrier particles, or bosons. Particles transfer energy between themselves by transferring bosons. Each fundamental force has its own corresponding boson – the strong force is carried by the gluon, the electromagnetic force is carried by the photon, and weak force is carried by the W and Z bosons. There is a theoretical graviton, responsible for gravity, but that has not yet been discovered.

The Standard Model is a form of a Grand Unified Theory as it can explain how all the fundamental forces apart from gravity affect particles, but it does not unite them as one force.

Incomplete picture

It is acknowledged that the Standard Model doesn't answer all the known questions about the Universe, but it's an excellent stepping stone to the new physics that may help us. Together with the new experiments being run at the Large Hadron Collider (LHC) at CERN in Geneva, we might soon find the missing pieces!

Surfing the Wave

Throw a rock into a pond and it will create ripples moving out from where the stone entered the water. In a similar way, large colliding masses should send gravitational waves into space. These invisible ripples in the very fabric of space would cause it to stretch and squeeze back again.

 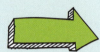 

On 11 February 2016, after decades of trying to directly detect such waves, physicists announced that they appear to have found them. The waves came from another galaxy around 1 billion light years away. There, two black holes collided, shaking the fabric of space and time, or *spacetime*. Here on Earth, two giant detectors in different parts of the United States quivered as the gravity waves passed through them.

Testing predications

In his theory of general relativity, Albert Einstein predicted that ripples in spacetime should radiate energy away from enormously violent events, such as colliding stars and black holes. Such events are immensely powerful, but the ripples they produce are extremely faint. By the time they reach Earth they compress spacetime by as little as the width of a proton. The newly found waves were picked up by the recently upgraded Laser Interferometer Gravitational-Wave Observatory (LIGO).

Spotting invisible ripples

To spot a signal, LIGO uses a special mirror to split a beam of laser light. The mirror sends each beam down one of two 4km-long tubes, which sit at right angles to each other. Light travels back and forth 400 times down each tunnel in the detector. This turns each beam's journey into a 1,600km round trip, before the two beams are put back together near where they were split.

4 km!

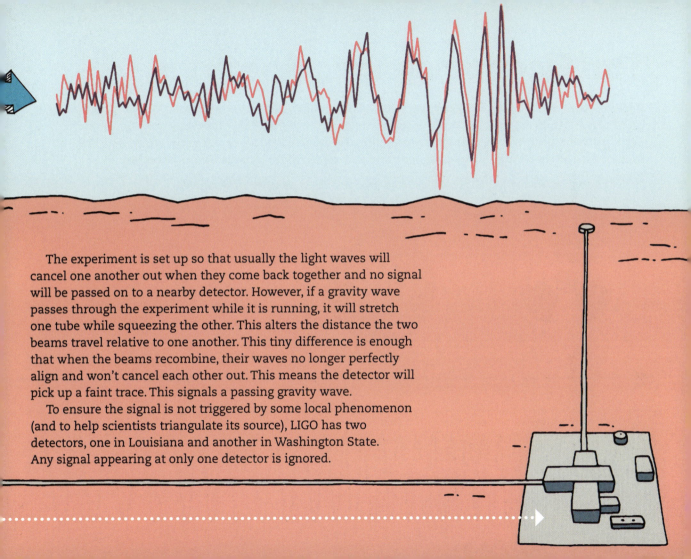

The experiment is set up so that usually the light waves will cancel one another out when they come back together and no signal will be passed on to a nearby detector. However, if a gravity wave passes through the experiment while it is running, it will stretch one tube while squeezing the other. This alters the distance the two beams travel relative to one another. This tiny difference is enough that when the beams recombine, their waves no longer perfectly align and won't cancel each other out. This means the detector will pick up a faint trace. This signals a passing gravity wave.

To ensure the signal is not triggered by some local phenomenon (and to help scientists triangulate its source), LIGO has two detectors, one in Louisiana and another in Washington State. Any signal appearing at only one detector is ignored.

The Electromagnetic Spectrum

Radio waves, microwaves, infrared radiation, visible light, ultraviolet radiation, X-rays, gamma rays. You might have heard of some or all of these, but did you know that they are all forms of light, just with different energies? Together they form the electromagnetic spectrum, and they make up all of the different forms of light that are given off by objects in our Universe.

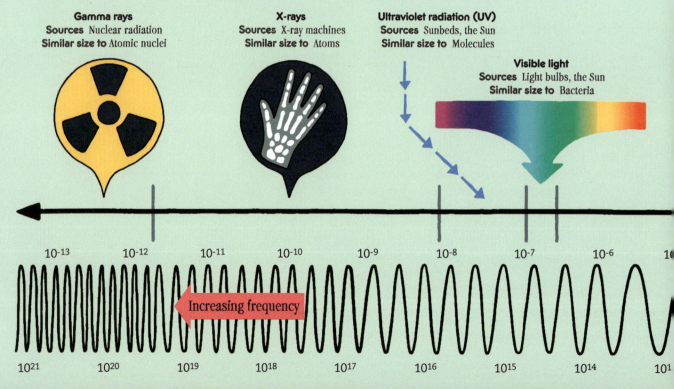

Gamma rays
Sources Nuclear radiation
Similar size to Atomic nuclei

X-rays
Sources X-ray machines
Similar size to Atoms

Ultraviolet radiation (UV)
Sources Sunbeds, the Sun
Similar size to Molecules

Visible light
Sources Light bulbs, the Sun
Similar size to Bacteria

10^{-13} 10^{-12} 10^{-11} 10^{-10} 10^{-9} 10^{-8} 10^{-7} 10^{-6} 10^{-5}

Increasing frequency

10^{21} 10^{20} 10^{19} 10^{18} 10^{17} 10^{16} 10^{15} 10^{14} 10^{1}

We can only see visible light with our eyes, but we use the whole of the spectrum in everyday life, from turning on the TV to looking at broken bones at the hospital.

We talk about the electromagnetic spectrum in terms of its wavelength, the length of one wave. The longer the wavelength, the less energy the waves have: radio waves have the longest wavelength and least energy, while gamma rays have the shortest wavelength and most energy. Frequency is the number of waves that pass a point every second. Frequency and wavelength are linked: the longer the wavelength, the lower the frequency.

All waves in the electromagnetic spectrum travel at the same speed: the speed of light!

Microwaves
Sources Microwave ovens, radar
Similar size to Grains of sugar

Radio waves
Sources Radio and TV signals, mobile phones, Wi-Fi signals
Similar size to Buildings

Infrared radiation (IR)
Sources Radar, people, the Sun
Similar size to Microbes

| 10^{-4} | 10^{-3} | 10^{-2} | 10^{-1} | 1 | 10 | 10^{2} | 10^{3} Wavelength (m) |

Increasing wavelength

| 10^{12} | 10^{11} | 10^{10} | 10^{9} | 10^{8} | 10^{7} | 10^{6} | 10^{5} Frequency (Hz) |

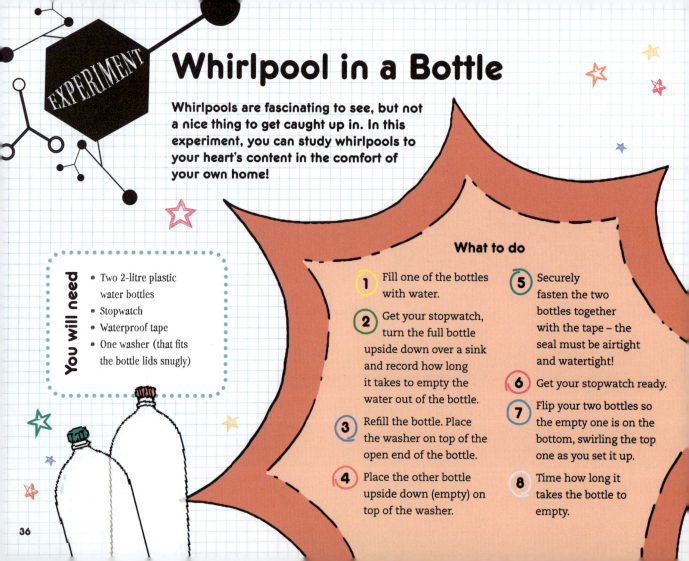

Whirlpool in a Bottle

Whirlpools are fascinating to see, but not a nice thing to get caught up in. In this experiment, you can study whirlpools to your heart's content in the comfort of your own home!

EXPERIMENT

You will need

- Two 2-litre plastic water bottles
- Stopwatch
- Waterproof tape
- One washer (that fits the bottle lids snugly)

What to do

1. Fill one of the bottles with water.

2. Get your stopwatch, turn the full bottle upside down over a sink and record how long it takes to empty the water out of the bottle.

3. Refill the bottle. Place the washer on top of the open end of the bottle.

4. Place the other bottle upside down (empty) on top of the washer.

5. Securely fasten the two bottles together with the tape – the seal must be airtight and watertight!

6. Get your stopwatch ready.

7. Flip your two bottles so the empty one is on the bottom, swirling the top one as you set it up.

8. Time how long it takes the bottle to empty.

It can be difficult to get the set-up right, but keep trying. What do you notice about the differences in the two times you measured? Which one was quicker?

DO TRY THIS AT HOME

Try this with different-sized bottles. You will always need two of the same size, but see if you always observe this effect. Try different ways to swirl the bottles as you turn them. Which way gives the quickest time?

How it works

Gravity is pulling the water down, but giving the water that initial swirl starts a spiralling drainage pattern, the same effect seen when cold air falls in a swirl as warm air rises – as in a tornado!

The reason this drains faster is because, if you look closely, you can see that throughout the whole process there is a hole where the air can flow up, surrounded by draining water. This makes for a much faster drainage than the traditional glug-glug of pouring from bottles. The glug-glug comes from the water and air having to both use the same passage; when the air is rising, the water ceases flowing and vice versa. This makes for slower drainage than the continuous vortex.

Mirror, Mirror, on the Wall

What is it about objects that let us see them? How do you see a tree, or a pencil, or this book? Most objects in the Universe don't emit light, so in order to see them they must reflect it instead. The walls in the room that you are in don't emit their own light; you can see them because they reflect the light from the ceiling lights overhead or from the Sun coming in through the window.

Hee hee!

All things reflected

Highly polished metal surfaces reflect light much like the silver layer in a mirror. A beam of light that falls onto the metal surface is reflected.

The process of reflection always involves two rays – an incoming or incident ray and an outgoing or reflected ray. The law of reflection requires that two rays are at identical angles but on opposite sides of the *normal* (an imaginary line at right angles to the mirror located at the point where the rays meet).

All things equal

All reflected light obeys the relationship that the *angle of incidence* equals the *angle of reflection*. Just as images are reflected from the surface of a mirror, light reflected from a smooth water surface also produces a clear image. A clear image is produced because all of the rays are reflected in the same direction by the very flat surface. When the surface of the water is wind-blown and irregular, the rays of light are reflected in many directions. The law of reflection is still obeyed, but, as the surface is not flat, the rays will hit different sections of the surface that will all be pointing in different directions. So the outgoing rays are reflected at many different angles and the image is disturbed. This is the reason why some objects appear matt (non-shiny), even though the surface seems flat. You would need to use a powerful microscope to see the true, bumpy surface of the object.

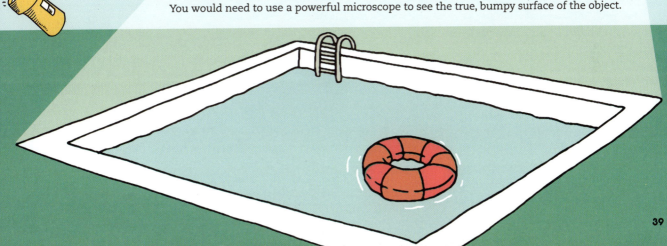

Bending Light

Light waves travel in straight lines through empty space, but more interesting things happen to them when they travel through other materials, particularly when they move from one material to another. That's not unusual: we do the same thing ourselves.

Have you noticed how your body slows down when you try to run through water? You can race across the sand at top speed but as soon as you hit the sea you slow right down. No matter how hard you try, you can't run as quickly through water as you could across the beach. The dense liquid is harder to push out of the way than air, so it slows you down. Exactly the same thing happens to light if you shine it into water or another dense material: it slows down, often quite dramatically. This change of speed makes the rays bend, a process called refraction.

Hi! I'm feeling a little detached right now.

How does it work?

Imagine driving a tank with caterpillar tracks along a field. If the field is just grass, the tank will zoom along. But what happens if the tank hits some mud? If the tank hits the mud at an angle, one side of the tank will hit the mud first. The track on this side will slip in the mud and won't move across the ground as easily as the track still on the grass, so the tank will turn towards the mud. Once both tracks are in the mud the tank will move along straight, but at a slower speed than before. On leaving the mud the track that leaves the mud first will have more grip and be able to move quicker than the track still stuck in the mud, so the tank will turn away from the mud. Once both tracks have left the mud, the tank will run straight.

If the tank hits the mud straight on, both tracks would hit the mud at the same time, so the tank won't change direction, just travel at a slower speed. This is a good way of thinking about how light behaves as it moves through different materials, and explains why objects put in water can look bent.

Bendy straws, bendy people

You've probably noticed that water can bend light. You can see this for yourself by putting a straw in a glass of water. Notice how the straw appears to kink at the point where the water meets the air above it. The bending happens not in the water itself but at the junction of the air and the water. You can see the same thing by looking at somebody in a clear-sided swimming pool; their head looks removed from their body!

Seeing Through the Gaps

Have you ever been to a harbour and watched the waves come in? You'll see that as the waves come through the gap they stop travelling straight, instead spreading out from the opening to form a series of curves, bending round to touch the harbour walls. The larger the waves are, the more they will curve. They curve most when the wavelength of the wave is the same size as the gap.

Spreading light

It might not be as visible, but the same thing happens with light. In order to see this effect, though, you need an opening that is a similar size to the wavelength. This is easy with sound or water waves, but with light the opening needs to be around 0.0000005m. You can see this effect, which is called diffraction, if you screw your eyes up and look at a streetlight in the dark. As your eyes close, the light seems to spread out in strange stripes as it squeezes through the narrow gaps between your eyelashes. The tighter you close your eyes, the more the light spreads (until it disappears when you close your eyes completely).

Finely grated

Diffraction becomes more interesting when we have multiple gaps that the light can travel through. When this happens, the light will create an interference pattern, formed of areas of bright light where the waves add together, and areas of darkness where the waves cancel each other out. The object used to do this is called a diffraction grating and it can have anywhere between a few gaps per mm to thousands of gaps per mm. A diffraction grating is an immensely useful tool to separate the light given off by electrons moving inside atoms. Each atom has a set range of wavelengths that it will give off as its electrons move around and, using a diffraction grating, physicists can study the light given off by objects such as stars to find out what elements they contain.

Get Physical!

All types of waves can be diffracted. X-ray diffraction is used to find out the atomic structure of objects and was essential to working out the structure of DNA!

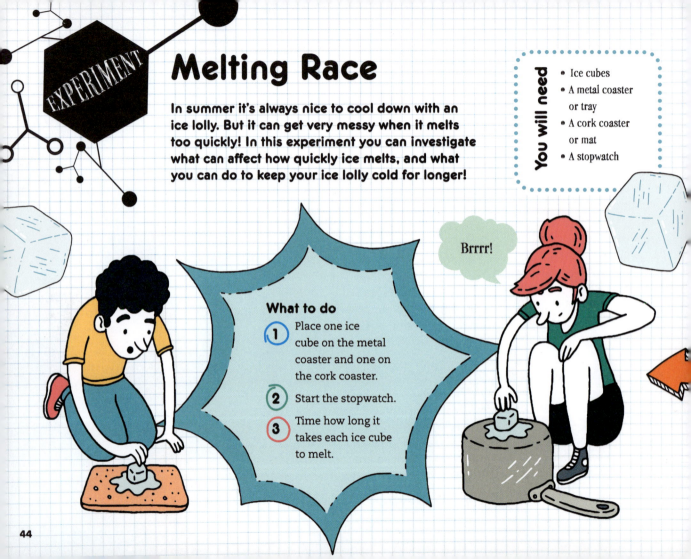

EXPERIMENT

Melting Race

In summer it's always nice to cool down with an ice lolly. But it can get very messy when it melts too quickly! In this experiment you can investigate what can affect how quickly ice melts, and what you can do to keep your ice lolly cold for longer!

You will need
- Ice cubes
- A metal coaster or tray
- A cork coaster or mat
- A stopwatch

Brrrr!

What to do

1. Place one ice cube on the metal coaster and one on the cork coaster.

2. Start the stopwatch.

3. Time how long it takes each ice cube to melt.

How it works

Heat energy will always move from high energy (high temperature) to low energy (low temperature), but some materials are better at transferring heat energy than others. If a material is good at transferring heat energy we say it is a good thermal conductor, if it is bad we say it is a good thermal insulator. In our everyday lives we want a mixture of insulators and conductors, depending on what we want to do. To stay warm outside we will wear a jacket, and if it is really cold we might wear a down jacket. Down is an excellent thermal insulator and will stop the hot air around you from escaping. Radiators are an example of a thermal conductor, as we want the heat to leave the radiator and heat the room.

As the ice cubes are melting, touch the coasters. You should notice that the metal coaster feels much, much colder than the cork coaster. The ice cube on the metal coaster will melt far more quickly than the one on the cork coaster, and will melt even quicker if you hold the coaster in your hands.

Try this experiment with as many different materials as you can find. Try paper, wool, a glass, a glass filled with water, your hand . . . Which one is the quickest? Which one is the slowest? Can you find the best thermal insulator and thermal conductor in your house?

DO TRY THIS AT HOME !

Radioactivity

The elements in the periodic table aren't always identical to each other, even if they have the same name. Sometimes elements have the same number of protons and electrons, but a different number of neutrons. These are called isotopes.

In the late nineteenth century, scientists discovered something very unexpected about certain isotopes. Throughout time, the atoms of these isotopes had been shooting off particles and emitting radiation without anyone suspecting that this was happening.

The scientists also found that nothing could be done to change what was emitted. The application of heat, electricity or any other force made no difference whatsoever. The emission seemed to be an unchangeable property of the substances. This emission is called radioactive decay.

Three different types
There are three different types of radioactive decay:

1. **Alpha decay** This is the heaviest form of decay, and is made up of two protons and two neutrons. As it is very positively charged, it can cause a lot of damage to humans if it gets inside the body.
2. **Beta decay** This is when a neutron in the nucleus turns into a proton and an electron. The electron can stay in the nucleus and is ejected from the atom.
3. **Gamma decay** This decay is a form of high-energy radiation and does not change the mass or the structure of the atom.

Oh dear, Tiddles! Have you been playing with your radioactive pal again?

For the greater good

While the different types of radioactive decay can be dangerous in different ways, there are also lots of ways it can be useful. A special use of the radioactive element uranium led to the development of nuclear energy. Doctors have also found that gamma rays can pass through living tissues for short distances and affect the tissue cells. They can disrupt chemical bonds in the molecules of important chemicals within cells, and so they help in treating cancers and other diseases.

Geologists have learned how to use radioactivity to determine the age of rocks and fossils. From this they obtain new checks on the ages of mountain ranges and how life on Earth has changed over time. The study of radioactivity continues to contribute to the understanding of the nature of atoms; from this, scientists are learning how energy and matter interact to bring about everything that happens in the physical universe.

Edison, Swan and the Light Bulb

The American inventor Thomas Edison (1847–1931) is often thought of as the inventor of the electric light bulb, but actually it was a British inventor called Joseph Swan who made the largest advances in producing the incandescent light bulb (light bulbs that glow by heating a thin filament in a vacuum tube) and lit up the first buildings in the world with electricity.

Light in the darkness

Humphry Davy, an English scientist, had invented the first light from electricity, the arc light, in 1800, but it wasn't practical for general use. This is where Joseph Swan comes in. Swan was a chemist working on photography paints who enjoyed experimenting with building a practical light source in his spare time. He worked on his design throughout the 1850s, and by 1860 he had built a working device and was awarded his first patent for his work (patents protect inventions so that nobody can steal them and claim them for their own).

In 1879 Swan gave a lecture in Newcastle, where his bulbs lit up the first public building in the world with electric lighting. Shortly after this Swan cleverly installed his bulbs in the house of Lord Armstrong, one of the most influential men in Britain, who showcased Swan's invention to the world's elite. Soon Swan had his own company, which was producing light bulbs commercially by 1881.

In December 1881 Swan's electric lighting was used to light the stage of the Savoy Theatre, and within a few years the Savoy became the first public building in the world to be completely lit by electricity.

Gentlemen, gentlemen! Why not combine your efforts?

Across the pond

At the same time, over in America, Thomas Edison was developing his own electric light bulb independently from Swan. Edison's work was about a year behind Swan's, and it took a while for news of the Englishman's invention to filter over to the US. This meant that during the period 1880–83 Edison was awarded and then stripped of a patent for his work. After a few legal arguments with Swan over who had invented the light bulb first, Swan and Edison merged their companies to form Edison and Swan, a company that lasted until 1964 making 'Ediswan' incandescent light bulbs.

I think you'll find it was me who got there first!

I thought it was me, pal!

Get Physical!

In November 1882 the Savoy staged Gilbert & Sullivan's *Iolanthe*, a comic opera about fairies, and Swan's company equipped the fairy actresses with incandescent star lights run by a small battery hidden in their hair – real fairy lights!

Under Pressure

Have you ever accidentally stood on a Lego brick? It really hurts, doesn't it? This is because all of your weight presses down through the tiny area of the brick, putting lots of pressure on the brick and causing a huge pain in your foot!

Pressure is measured as the force you use divided by the area over which you use it. If you use a bigger force (e.g. if an adult steps on the brick instead of you), or if you use the same force over a smaller area (you step on an even smaller piece of Lego), you increase the pressure. We experience different types of pressure all the time.

&:%$@!!!
Who left that there?!

Air pressure

You may not think it, but air actually weighs quite a lot. The gases in the Earth's atmosphere are made up of tiny molecules that are constantly crashing into your body and trying to press it down and inwards. Usually you have about the weight of a small car pressing down on you all the time, just from the air above your head!

This pressing force is called air pressure. It is greatest at ground level, where there are the most air molecules. At greater heights there are fewer air molecules and the air pressure is much lower. It is possible to compress (squeeze) air, and this is used to inflate vehicle tyres and to power machines such as pneumatic drills. There's an experiment on air pressure on page 58.

Get Physical!

The deepest that anybody has dived to with no specialist equipment is 122m. The deepest anybody has managed to get is 10,911m at the bottom of Challenger Deep in the Mariana Trench, which was first reached in 1960 in a specially designed vessel that had walls nearly 15cm thick!

Water pressure

Water behaves differently from air when it's under pressure. It cannot be compressed, and this makes it useful for transmitting force in machines, using a system called hydraulics. Water is also heavier than air, and an increase in water pressure affects humans more than a change in air pressure. Even with a snorkel or other breathing apparatus, it feels much harder to breathe underwater. The water above you presses down from all sides on your body, so your lungs find it harder to expand to take in air. The deeper you go, the more water there is above you and the greater the pressure on your body.

Static Shock

Have you ever touched something and got a shock from it? Chances are that was an electric shock caused by static electricity. Static electricity is the build-up of electrical charge on an object's surface. It is called 'static' because the charges are stationary, staying still rather than moving or flowing around.

We can see static electricity every day and it can even build up on us! For example, when you rub a balloon on your head and you lift it, your hair sticks to it. You can sometimes feel it when you remove your sweater. One of the most powerful and well-known forms of static electricity is lightning, where the charges build up between clouds and discharge to the ground as a lightning bolt!

Charges, charges everywhere

Earlier you learned that atoms are made up of neutrons, protons and electrons, with the protons and neutrons forming the nucleus in the middle and the electrons spinning around the outside. A static charge is formed when two surfaces touch each other and the electrons move from one object to another. One object will have a positive charge, as it has fewer electrons than before, and the other a negative charge, as it gains electrons. Rubbing the items quickly, like when you rub a balloon fast over your hair or your feet on the carpet, will build up a large charge. Items with different charges (positive and negative) will attract, while items with similar charges (both positive or both negative) will push away from each other. Your hair sticks to the balloon because the friction that builds up as you rub them against each other causes a positive charge to be built up on your hair and a negative charge to build up on the balloon. Since each hair has the same charge, they all try to push away from each other, but at the same time will be attracted to the negative balloon. So your hair will fan out and stick to the balloon.

Useful charges

Static electricity is actually really useful in many different industries. In printers and photocopiers, static charges are used to attract the special ink to the paper. Other uses include paint sprayers, air filters, and dust removal.

Get Physical!

Static electricity can also cause damage. Some electronic chips, especially those in computers, are very sensitive to static electricity, and special protections have been developed so that they aren't exposed to any unexpected shocks!

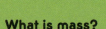

Searching for the Higgs Boson

Physicists are always trying to simplify the Universe, to explain it as elegantly as possible, using maths to form equations instead of long written explanations. Throughout this book there are examples of physicists forming theories about the world around them, based on their observations and experiences.
However, sometimes these explanations fall short and we can't explain what we see.

What is mass?

Nearly a half-century ago, Peter Higgs and a handful of other physicists were trying to understand the origin of a basic physical feature: mass. At a microscopic level, an object's mass comes from its atoms, which are themselves built from fundamental particles, electrons and quarks. But where do the masses of these and other fundamental particles come from? The Standard Model does not explain mass. When the physicists initially modelled the behaviour of the fundamental particles, they found a puzzle. If they excluded mass from their calculations, the equations worked perfectly, but they knew the particles did have mass. If they tried to account for the mass the equations fell apart, and when they did manage to solve them they were complex and inconsistent.

The Higgs field

Here's the idea put forward by Higgs: don't include mass in the equations. Keep the equations perfect and symmetric, and instead consider them working in a strange environment. Imagine that all of space is uniformly filled with an invisible substance – now called the Higgs field – that affects all particles that move through it by applying a drag force to them. If you try to increase the speed of a particle, according to Higgs, you would feel this drag force as a resistance. In this case, you would interpret the resistance to the change in speed that you feel as the particle's mass. As an example, think of a weighted brick at the bottom of a swimming pool. When you push on the brick, it will feel much more massive than it does outside of water. The way it interacts with the water has effectively given it more mass. It is the same with particles submerged in the Higgs field.

Discovering the Higgs particle

The Large Hadron Collider (LHC) is a machine that smashes protons together to discover smaller particles. Its main goal has been to try to find the elusive Higgs particle – the Higgs boson – and it has been upgraded several times to search for it. In 2012, physicists from the LHC stunned the world by announcing they had discovered the Higgs particle, and Peter Higgs was awarded the Nobel Prize in 2013.

55

It's All Relative

In 1887, two scientists, Michelson and Morley, wanted to measure how fast the Earth was moving through space, and to do this they were measuring the speed of light.

To understand why they decided to do that, think about it like this. Imagine you're in a rainstorm with the wind blowing against your back. If you started running, the rain wouldn't hit your back as hard. It would be travelling slower compared to you. Scientists would say that the rain was travelling slower *relative* to you. And, of course, if you turned around and ran towards the rain, it would hit you even harder than if you stood still. Scientists would say that the rain was moving faster *relative* to you.

Back then, scientists thought that light acted like raindrops in a storm. They thought that if the Earth was moving around the Sun, and the Sun was moving around the galaxy, they should be able to measure how fast they were moving through space. All they would need to do was measure how the speed of light changed.

And that's exactly what they did. But they discovered something very strange.

The speed of light was the same no matter what. It didn't matter which direction they were travelling around the Sun.

The absolute speed limit

The scientists had discovered that light didn't act like raindrops, or like anything else in the Universe. No matter how fast you were moving, and no matter what direction you were heading, the speed of light was always the same. This was very unexpected, and it took Albert Einstein, with his theory of special relativity, to figure out how this could be.

Tommy, it's never going to fit!

Timey-wimey

Einstein figured out that there was only one way to explain how things could work out this way: it was only possible if time slowed down.

So let's go back to our rainstorm. How could it be possible for the rain to feel exactly the same, even if you were running through it? Well, if you ran away from the rain, and your time slowed down, the rain would seem like it was speeding up. It would feel like it was hitting your back at exactly the same speed.

Scientists call this *time dilation*. No matter how fast you're moving, your time slows down so that you measure the speed of light to be exactly the same.

Get Physical!

At really high speeds, length is also affected, with objects appearing shorter than they are. If a spaceship 100m long was flying by you at half the speed of light, it would appear to be 87m long. If it speeded up to 95 per cent of the speed of light, it would only appear to be 31m long! Of course, this is all relative. To people on board the spaceship, it would always appear to be 100m long.

Trust me!

Google 'pole-barn paradox' to see how you can fit the ladder into the barn!

Collapsing Bottles

Have you ever wanted to be able to impress your friends with a clever science trick? With this quick experiment you can demonstrate the power of physics with unbelievable results!

You will need

- A kettle
- A large 2-litre plastic bottle
- Oven gloves
- Depending on your age, you may need an adult to help with handling the hot water

What to do

1. Boil some water in the kettle.

2. Unscrew the lid from the bottle.

3. Once it has boiled, very carefully pour some hot water into the bottle.

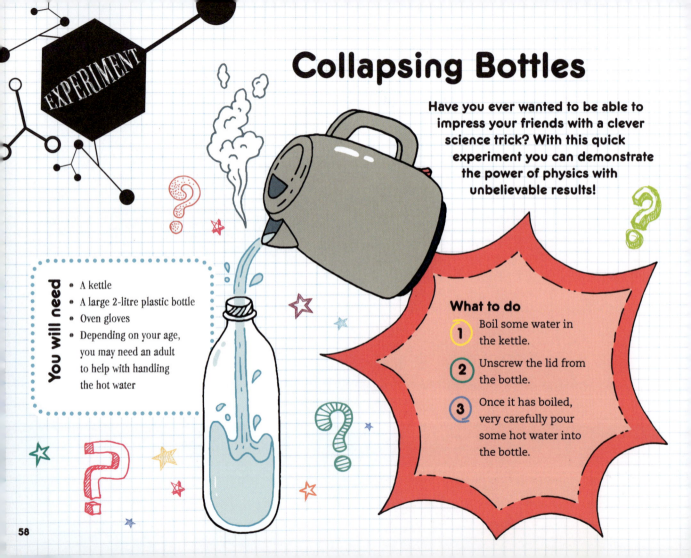

How it works

The hot water gives the air in the bottle energy. This means that the pressure inside the bottle increases as the molecules have more energy. This extra energy will also allow some of the molecules to escape. Once the hot water has been poured out, the air particles begin to cool. As they cool they lose energy and stop moving around as much, making the pressure inside the bottle drop to below the pressure outside. Because the top is screwed on, no particles can enter the bottle. The result is that the air pressing on the outside causes the bottle to collapse until the pressure on the inside matches that on the outside.

4. Using the oven gloves, slowly swirl the water and pour it out down the sink.

5. As soon as the bottle is empty, tightly replace the cap.

6. Sit back and watch.

The bottle should collapse in on itself after a few minutes.

DO TRY THIS AT HOME

Try the experiment with different bottles. Which one works best? Does the amount of hot water or the way you pour it out make any difference to the outcome? Try and find the method that makes the bottle collapse the quickest!

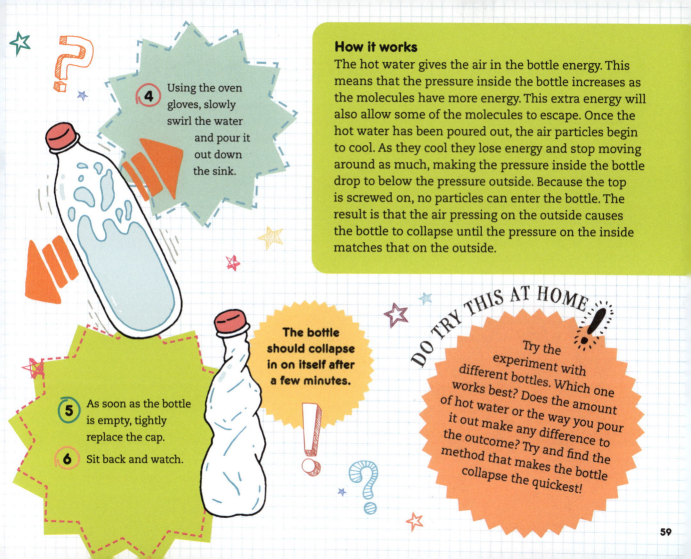

The Marksman and the Monkey

In order to help themselves and others to understand a tricky topic, scientists often come up with thought experiments to explain their ideas. These experiments aren't really carried out, just described in order to see what will happen.

This particular thought experiment looks at a pretty well-understood but still confusing topic: gravity.

Imagine a marksman has been called into a zoo to tranquillise a monkey who needs treatment. When the marksman arrives, he spots the monkey hanging from a branch at the far end of his enclosure. But he knows that the monkey will reflexively drop from the branch immediately after he pulls the trigger. So, as soon as the dart leaves the barrel, the monkey will be in free fall, heading to the ground.

Choices, choices

However, the marksman doesn't know exactly how fast the tranquilliser dart will travel after leaving the gun – he just knows it'll move fast. With all of this in mind, where should he aim? Where would you aim?

There are three choices:

1 Aim **above** the monkey

2 Aim **directly at** the monkey

3 Aim **below** the monkey

Intuitively, you might think that he needs to aim below the monkey, as the dart will move very fast. If he shoots at or above it, the dart may whizz over its head and be lost. But that's wrong.

The correct answer is…

2 Aim directly at the monkey

Once the dart has left the gun, there's only one main force acting on it: gravity (the air resistance is not enough to affect its movement). Equally, gravity will be the only force to act on the monkey once it lets go.

The constant acceleration due to gravity affects both the monkey and the dart in the same way. As a result, the dart will fall a little bit below where the marksman initially aimed. By the time the dart travels 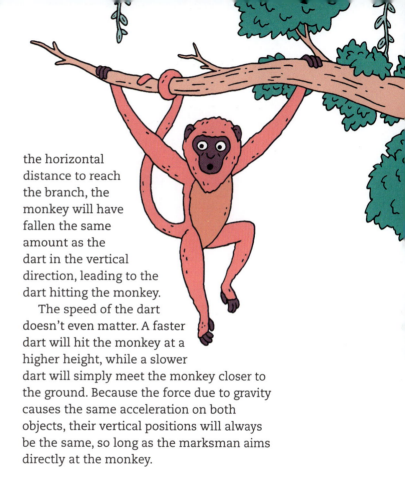 the horizontal distance to reach the branch, the monkey will have fallen the same amount as the dart in the vertical direction, leading to the dart hitting the monkey.

The speed of the dart doesn't even matter. A faster dart will hit the monkey at a higher height, while a slower dart will simply meet the monkey closer to the ground. Because the force due to gravity causes the same acceleration on both objects, their vertical positions will always be the same, so long as the marksman aims directly at the monkey.

Famous Physicists II

Be less curious about people and more curious about ideas.

Marie Curie (1867–1934)

Marie Curie was a Polish-born physicist and chemist who conducted ground-breaking research on radioactivity. She was the first woman to win a Nobel Prize (in Physics in 1903 for her work on radioactivity, along with her husband Pierre Curie and Henri Becquerel). She also became the first person (and only woman) to be awarded a second Nobel Prize, and is the only person to be awarded Nobel Prizes in multiple sciences, when she was awarded the Nobel Prize for Chemistry in 1911 for her discovery of the elements polonium and radium.

Marie Curie died from a rare blood disease caused by her exposure to radiation. At the time the dangers of radiation were not understood, and now all of her notes from the 1890s are too dangerous to touch due to their high levels of radioactivity, even down to her cookbooks!

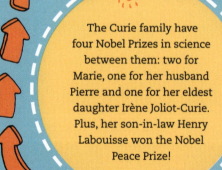

Get Physical!

The Curie family have four Nobel Prizes in science between them: two for Marie, one for her husband Pierre and one for her eldest daughter Irène Joliot-Curie. Plus, her son-in-law Henry Labouisse won the Nobel Peace Prize!

Lise Meitner (1878–1968)

Lise Meitner was an Austrian-born physicist whose ground-breaking work into the mechanisms of radioactivity helped to explain the process of nuclear fission. Although she was not awarded a Nobel Prize for her work, she is one of the most important scientists to work in the field of radioactivity and nuclear physics. She is also credited with the discovery of the element protactinium.

She was invited to become part of the Manhattan Project in 1942, to work on the creation of the atomic bomb, but she refused the position because she did not want to build weapons. She died in 1968 in the UK at the age of 89, and was still giving lectures and visiting universities well into her eighties.

> I will have nothing to do with a bomb!

> Science is a quest for understanding.

Jocelyn Bell Burnell (1943–)

British astrophysicist Jocelyn Bell Burnell is a modern trailblazer for female astronomers, and discovered pulsars while still a PhD student at the University of Cambridge in 1967. In 1974 her supervisors were awarded the Nobel Prize for the discovery, but Jocelyn missed out. Today Jocelyn is still an active researcher, travelling the world giving talks on her work, and campaigns strongly to get more women involved in science.

Making a Pinhole Camera

Would you like to make a wonderful camera in just five minutes? Don't worry, it's easy to make, plus you will be able to see everything (including your family) upside down! Just follow the instructions below, and before you know it you'll be looking at the world in a whole new way.

You will need

- An empty, clean Pringles tube
- Pen/pencil
- Stanley knife (depending on your age, this may need to be used by an adult)
- Sticky tape
- Foil
- Drawing pin

What to do

1. Take the lid off the Pringles tube.

2. Draw a line all the way around the tube, at about 8cm from the bottom.

3. Very carefully cut along this line all the way around the tube – mind your fingers!

4. Take the lid and place it over the cut end on the bottom part of the tube.

5. Get the other piece of the tube and place that back on top of the lid as it was before; it should now look like the original tube with the lid in the middle.

6. Use the tape to stick it all together, but only put tape on the outside of the tube.

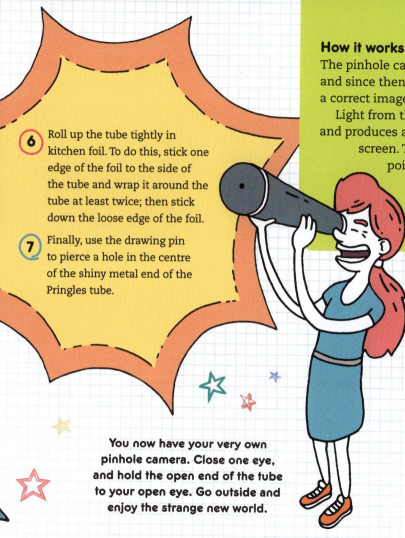

6 Roll up the tube tightly in kitchen foil. To do this, stick one edge of the foil to the side of the tube and wrap it around the tube at least twice; then stick down the loose edge of the foil.

7 Finally, use the drawing pin to pierce a hole in the centre of the shiny metal end of the Pringles tube.

You now have your very own pinhole camera. Close one eye, and hold the open end of the tube to your open eye. Go outside and enjoy the strange new world.

How it works

The pinhole camera was first used in about 1000BC, and since then it has been a simple way of producing a correct image of a scene.

Light from the object goes through the pinhole and produces an upside-down image in colour on the screen. This is because only light from one point on the object can reach a given point on the screen. There is no need for a lens as the pinhole acts as a lens, so the camera is always in focus.

The size of the pinhole is very important and will affect the image that is made. Build several cameras and try different-sized holes – you can even make multiple holes! How does this affect the image? Which ones work best?

DO TRY THIS AT HOME

Black Bodies and Quantum Physics

If you bake a cake in the oven it heats up as it cooks – leave it in there too long and it will burn and turn black. If the oven is hot enough it might even catch fire! At whatever point you take it out of the oven, you can feel the heat coming off it: the hotter the oven is, the hotter the cake is. Physicists say that the cake is radiating (giving off) energy in the form of heat.

Measuring energy

If you had a device to measure all the radiation coming off the cake, you would find that while most of the radiation emitted would match its temperature, there would also be other energies given off from other parts of the electromagnetic spectrum. This is called the object's spectrum, and for a while the spectrum of a hot object couldn't be explained with physics.

Breaking physics

In order to solve this puzzle, physicists used a thought experiment. They imagined a *black body*, an object that just absorbs light: it doesn't reflect anything and so appears completely black. A black body just radiates at its given temperature and doesn't lose any energy; it's the perfect hot object. When the spectrum for the black body was created, every attempt to explain it with classical physics went wrong.

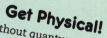

Get Physical!

Without quantum physics, the Sun would explode. If energy wasn't quantised, classical physics says that the Sun should give off infinite amounts of high-energy light and tear itself apart!

The birth of quantum physics

This idea was revolutionary. Planck said that the energy in a body couldn't just take on any value; instead it could only take specific, *quantised* values. This idea that all energy could be broken down and quantised led to the birth of quantum physics, and to understanding what's going on inside atoms.

Discretely changing physics

Classical physics says that energy is continuous: it can have any value, and this was what was going wrong when physicists tried to explain black bodies. The German theoretical physicist Max Planck solved this problem by saying that energy couldn't be continuous, but it had to have *discrete* set values instead. If you limit the values that the energy can take, you can create the spectrum that is needed.

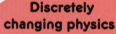

Nuclear Fission

Generating electricity is a huge business: every country in the world requires electricity, and the demand is growing every day.

Whether they are powered by coal, gas or nuclear energy, most power stations operate on the same principle. They heat up water and turn it into steam. The steam then turns a turbine, which in turn generates electricity. Nuclear power stations produce their energy through nuclear fission, the process of splitting an atom into smaller parts. This is actually a very rare process, as very few atoms go through fission under normal circumstances, and it can be difficult to achieve safely.

Special measures

The most well-known atom that undergoes fission is uranium 235 (U-235: a uranium isotope that has an atomic mass of 235). U-235 is not the only isotope of uranium – the most common isotope is U-238 – but it's the only one that undergoes fission. As the only isotope that can be used for nuclear fission, the U-235 atoms have to be separated from the more numerous U-238 atoms. The difficulty and cost of completing this separation is what has prevented most countries from having nuclear power (or from going on to develop nuclear weapons).

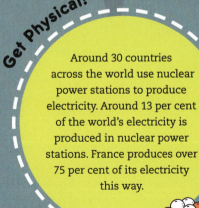

Get Physical!

Around 30 countries across the world use nuclear power stations to produce electricity. Around 13 per cent of the world's electricity is produced in nuclear power stations. France produces over 75 per cent of its electricity this way.

neutron

U-235 nucleus

U-235 nucleus splits into smaller nuclei and more neutrons

neutron

ENERGY

neutron

neutrons go on to hit more U-235 nuclei (chain reaction)

Making a chain

In a nuclear reaction, scientists shoot a whole bunch of neutrons at U-235 atoms. When one neutron hits the nucleus, the atom absorbs it and becomes U-236. A U-236 atom is unstable and will split apart. After it splits, it gives off three neutrons and a lot of energy. The energy goes into heating the water and turning it into steam, and the neutrons hit three other U-235 atoms in the area and cause them to become U-236. Each cycle, the reaction gets three times bigger.

A reaction that, once started, continues by itself is called a chain reaction. A chain reaction that keeps getting bigger is called an *uncontrolled* chain reaction. Left alone, and with sufficient U-235, the energy would grow large enough to cause a big explosion! To stop this happening, reactors contain moderators, which absorb some of the freed neutrons to *moderate* the rate of reaction and prevent it from getting out of control.

Nuclear Fusion

Nuclear fusion is the opposite of nuclear fission. In fission, a heavy nucleus is split into smaller nuclei, but in fusion, lighter nuclei are fused together to form a heavier nucleus.

The fusion process is the reaction that powers the Sun. On the Sun, in a series of nuclear reactions, four isotopes of hydrogen-1 (a proton and electron) are fused into helium-4, with the release of a tremendous amount of energy. The first demonstration of nuclear fusion by humans was the hydrogen bomb, initially built by the US military in 1952. A hydrogen bomb is approximately 1,000 times as powerful as an ordinary atomic bomb.

Current challenges

The goal of scientists for the last 50 years has been the controlled release of energy from a fusion reaction. If the energy from a fusion reaction can be released slowly, it can be used to produce electricity. It will provide an unlimited supply of energy that has no waste to deal with or contaminants to harm the atmosphere – simply non-polluting helium.

But achieving this goal requires overcoming three problems:

1 Temperature Fusion requires a huge amount of energy just to start. Heat is used to provide the energy, but it takes a *lot* of heat to start the reaction. Scientists estimate that the sample of hydrogen isotopes must be heated to approximately 40 million °C (hotter than the Sun's core!). So far nothing scientists have tried has come close to this temperature.

2 Time The charged nuclei must be held together close enough and long enough for the fusion reaction to start. Scientists estimate that the heated gas, or plasma, needs to be held together for about one second, which is much longer than they can currently do.

3 Containment There is not a material in existence that will stay whole at the temperatures required, so scientists have to look at other options. Because the plasma has a charge, magnetic fields can be used to contain it – like a magnetic bottle. But if the bottle leaks, the reaction won't take place, and scientists have yet to create a magnetic field that won't allow the plasma to leak.

Magnets

Magnets probably formed the starting point for one of the first science experiments you ever did: playing with fridge magnets, pulling them away from the fridge and seeing how close they had to be before they were pulled onto it. Magnets have been around and have been used for thousands of years, but it's only recently that scientists have understood how they work as they've learned about the structure of particles.

Magnetism is an invisible field caused by the properties of certain materials. In most objects, the electrons spin in different, random directions, which cause them to cancel out the forces each exert. However, magnets are different. Here molecules are uniquely arranged so that their electrons spin in the same direction. This arrangement of atoms creates two poles in a magnet, a north-seeking pole and a south-seeking pole.

I'm sorry, I'm just not attracted to you.

Get Physical!

Did you know the Earth is like a giant bar magnet due to its iron core? This is why we have a North Pole and a South Pole and can use the magnets in compasses to help us find them. Animals also use the Earth's magnetic field as a navigation aid, with whales and birds using them to find migration routes around the Earth.

Opposites attract

The magnetic force in a magnet flows from the north pole to the south pole, which in turn creates a magnetic field around a magnet. Have you ever held two magnets close to each other? When you try to push the south poles together, they will repel each other, as will two north poles. Turn one magnet around, and the north and the south poles will be attracted to each other.

Rare elements

Not many elements have the right kind of structure to allow the electrons to line up to create a magnet. The main material used for magnets is iron, but as steel has large amounts of iron in it, it can also be used. However, iron is not the only material that magnets can be made from: neodymium and samarium work too, and are called rare earth magnets.

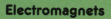

Electromagnets

Magnets can also be created using electricity. If a length of wire is coiled around an iron bar, it turns into a very strong magnet when current runs through the wire. If the current is turned off, the magnet turns off. This is called an electromagnet. They are used whenever magnets need to be turned on and off.

73

Measuring the Speed of Light

The speed of light is extremely quick and measuring it accurately is incredibly difficult. But, because microwaves travel at the speed of light, in this simple experiment you can calculate a value for the speed of light that should be close to the actual value using just your microwave!

You will need

- A microwave oven
- A piece of black card
- Mini marshmallows
- A ruler
- A pencil
- A calculator

What to do

1. Remove the plate from the microwave so that it doesn't rotate.

2. Rule a line across the middle of the black card with the pencil.

3. Place a row of mini-marshmallows along the line, end up; if they don't stay up use a bit of water to stick them down.

4. Carefully place the card in the microwave so that the marshmallows go across the microwave.

5. Close the microwave door and run at full power for 30 seconds.

6. Remove the card with the marshmallows on.

7. Look at the information sticker at the back on the microwave to find its operating frequency. It should be around 2,450MHz.

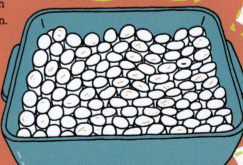

You should notice that some of your marshmallows have expanded and some haven't: the pattern should look like a wave. Measure the distance from the middle of one set of unaffected marshmallows to the next set of unaffected marshmallows. This will give you the distance of half a wavelength, so double it to give you a figure for a full wavelength. (If you measure in cm remember to divide by 100 to give you the figure in m.)

To work out the speed of the microwave waves we need to use the equation:

$$\text{Speed (in m/s)} = \text{frequency (in Hz)} \times \text{wavelength (in m)}$$

The frequency is the number you found on the back of the microwave (2,450MHz is actually 2,450,000,000Hz) and the wavelength is double the distance you measured. Use your calculator to multiply these two numbers together to calculate the speed of light. Turn to page 97 to see how you compare to the actual value!

How it works

A microwave cooks food by heating the water molecules inside the food using standing waves. Standing waves are formed when the waves are reflected on the metal sides of the microwave, and they create areas of high energy and areas of low energy. Because we removed the rotating plate, this effect is very obvious. This is the reason why you should always leave food in the microwave once the timer has stopped – certain parts of the food will be very hot and others will be cooler. It takes time for the energy to heat all the food up to the correct temperature.

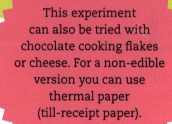

This experiment can also be tried with chocolate cooking flakes or cheese. For a non-edible version you can use thermal paper (till-receipt paper).

DO TRY THIS AT HOME

Temperature Scale

When talking about heat and energy, temperature is very important. But it can be measured in different ways. You may have heard of the Celsius scale, but did you know there's a Fahrenheit scale and a Kelvin scale too?

The classic Fahrenheit
This is the oldest temperature scale still in use, developed in 1774. Today this scale is mainly used in the USA and a few Pacific Islands.

The water scale
Celsius is the modern metric scale and is based around the measurements of water: 0°C for the melting point of water, 100°C for the boiling point of water. Celsius is the most common temperature scale in use today.

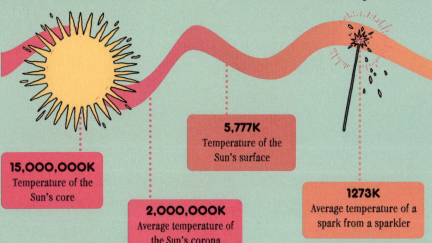

5,777K
Temperature of the Sun's surface

15,000,000K
Temperature of the Sun's core

2,000,000K
Average temperature of the Sun's corona

1273K
Average temperature of a spark from a sparkler

1123K
Average temperature of a campfire

373K (100°C, 212°F)
Boiling point of water

Going down

The Kelvin scale is the scale used by scientists and is actually the same as the Celsius scale, just with a different starting point. The only difference is that you can't have a negative temperature on the Kelvin scale: 0K – absolute zero – is the coldest temperature there is; nothing can be colder than it.

Measuring temperature

Even though scientists may use only a few scales to measure temperature, there are dozens of types of devices that measure temperatures. All these devices are called thermometers because they measure temperature. There are thermometers to measure your body temperature, the temperature in your oven, and even the temperature of liquid oxygen.

329.7K
(56.7°C, 134°F)
Highest recorded temperature on Earth, Death Valley, USA, July 1913

293K
(20°C, 68°F)
Room temperature

184K
(-89°C, -128.2°F)
Lowest recorded temperature, Vostok, Antarctica, July 1983

3K
(-270°C, -454°F)
Average temperature of space

310K
(37°C, 98.6°F)
Average human body temperature

273K
(0°C, 32°F)
Freezing point of water

77K
(-196°C, -321°F)
Boiling point of liquid nitrogen

0K
(-273.15°C, -459.5°F)
Absolute zero; lowest possible temperature in the Universe

Newton's Laws of Motion

Sir Isaac Newton has cropped up quite a lot already in this book. That's because he came up with many laws that describe the world of his time, and which are still relevant for the world we live in today. Here we are going to look more closely at his laws that describe how things move: Newton's three laws of motion.

First Law

An object at rest stays at rest, and an object in motion stays in motion, with the same direction and speed, unless acted on by an unbalanced force.

This means that if you are moving and nothing is happening to you, nothing will change – if you're going in a specific direction at a particular speed you will always go in that direction at that speed. Forever. If you aren't moving and nothing happens to you, you'll stay still. Forever.

This may sound a bit strange but, remember, in everyday life most of our movement is stopped by friction, so we are always trying to overcome it.

Second Law

$$F = ma$$
or
$$\text{Force} = \text{mass} \times \text{acceleration}$$

The second law says that resultant force on an object is directly related to its acceleration multiplied by its mass. So if you apply the same force to two objects with different masses, they will accelerate differently and will end up moving at different speeds. The smaller the object's mass is, the faster it will go.

Third Law

For every action (force) there is an equal and opposite reaction (force).

Usually, forces are found in pairs. Take sitting in a chair, for example. Your body exerts a force downwards and the chair needs to exert an equal force upwards, or the chair will collapse. If it exerts a force upwards greater than your weight, it will rise up off the floor! Another example is a rocket taking off. When the engines are fired, the force points down towards the ground. This creates a force that is equal, but in the opposite direction, that pushes the rocket up.

Rollercoaster Rides

We might not all be racing drivers or astronauts and not everyone can dive to the bottom of the sea or climb up Mount Everest. But we can all go on rollercoasters and see what it feels like to push ourselves to the limit.

Wheeeeeee!

Get Physical!

For the most exhilarating ride, sit at the back of the rollercoaster. This is where you are whipped over the top of the hills and have the biggest decelerations through the bottom of the hills, as it's where the forces change the quickest.

Where's the engine?

Have you ever noticed that rollercoasters don't have an engine? When they climb the first hill there is a winch pulling the cars up. This is usually the longest part of the ride – some rollercoasters are pulled 100m up in the air!

The winch uses energy to pull the rollercoasters up the hill, but that energy can't simply disappear. The rollercoaster cars store it just by being up in the air – and the higher up they are, the more energy they store. They'll use the same energy to race back down the hill when the ride begins. Because they have the *potential* to use that energy in the future, we call the energy they're storing gravitational potential energy.

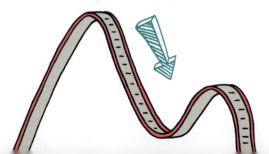

Going down!

When the car goes over the brow of the first hill, the force of gravity makes them hurtle downwards, so they accelerate. As they accelerate, their gravitational potential energy turns into kinetic energy. The further they go down the hill, the faster they go, and the more of their original potential energy is converted into kinetic energy.

At the start of the ride, the cars are said to have no gravitational potential energy with respect to the ride. Throughout the ride, they are constantly swapping back and forth between potential and kinetic energy. Each time they race up a hill, they gain more potential energy (by rising higher in the air), but they gain it by losing some kinetic energy too (by slowing down). That's why rollercoaster cars always go slower in the highest bits of a ride and faster in the low bits.

Forced into your seat

Energy is what makes a rollercoaster ride last, but the forces that you experience are what make it so thrilling. You can't see the forces pushing and pulling your body as you race around the track. But it's forces that knock you backwards, forwards and side to side, that make you feel as light as air one minute and as heavy as a rock the next. It's also forces that keep you safely in your seat when you're suddenly spinning upside down.

Cartesian Diver

This very simple experiment is named after the French scientist René Descartes, who used a very similar set-up to explain the Archimedes Principle and how gases behave.

You will need

- A clear 1-litre plastic bottle and cap (NOT a big 2-litre bottle)
- A ballpoint pen cap that doesn't have any holes in it (you can fill in/cover any holes with tape)
- Some modelling clay

What to do

1. Remove any labels from your bottle so you can watch the action.

2. Fill the bottle to the very top with water.

3. Place a pea-sized piece of modelling clay at the end of the point on the pen cap.

4. Slowly place the pen cap into the bottle, modelling clay end first (some water will spill out – that's OK); it should just barely float (if it sinks, take some clay away; if it floats too much, add more clay).

5. Now screw on the bottle cap nice and tight.

6. Now for the fun part. You can make the pen cap rise and fall at your command. Squeeze the bottle hard – the pen cap sinks. Stop squeezing and the pen cap rises. With a little practice, you can even get it to stop right in the middle.

How it works

Impressive, but how does it work? This experiment is all about density. When you squeeze the bottle, the air bubble in the pen cap is compressed and that makes it denser than the water around it. When this happens, the pen sinks. When you stop squeezing, the bubble gets bigger again, the water is forced out of the cap, and the pen cap rises.

If it doesn't work, play around with the amount of clay and be sure the bottle is filled to the very top before putting on the cap.

DO TRY THIS AT HOME

Ketchup diver

Next time you eat out, take one of the ketchup packets. Don't open it – just put it in the bottle the same way instead of the pen cap. When you squeeze the bottle the air bubble inside the packet compresses and become denser. The bubble in the packet makes it rise and fall just like the pen cap. Have fun!

To Wave or Not to Wave

The idea that light can behave both like a wave and a particle is perhaps one of the most confusing concepts in physics, because it is so unlike anything we see in the ordinary world.

Wave or particle?

Physicists who studied light in the eighteenth and nineteenth centuries had big arguments about whether light was made up of particles or waves. When they carried out experiments, light seemed to do both! Sometimes it would go in a straight line, like a particle, but other experiments found the wavelength of light and its frequency just like all other known waves.

It's...both?

In 1909, a scientist named Geoffrey Taylor borrowed an experiment invented earlier by Thomas Young, where light was shone through two small slits right next to each other. When bright light was shone through these two small slits, it created an interference pattern that seemed to show that light was actually a wave, because in some places the light waves cancelled each other out and in others they added together to make very bright areas, giving a pattern of light and dark patches.

Taylor's idea was to take a photo of the light coming out of the holes with a special camera that was unusually sensitive to light. Taylor turned down the light to a very dim level and started taking pictures. When he did this he found that, if the light was dim enough, he saw just two tiny slits of light coming through, just what was expected if light was a particle. But when Taylor exposed the camera for long enough, allowing enough of the dim light to pass through, the dots eventually filled up the photo to make an interference pattern again. This

Schrödinger's cat is a famous thought experiment about quantum mechanics, where a cat is said to be both alive and dead inside a box until it is observed. Physicists use Schrödinger's experiment to test new theories about quantum mechanics.

I'm very much alive, surely?

No, I think you're a goner, chum!

single experiment demonstrated that light was somehow *both* a wave *and* a particle.

This experiment has been repeated so often that physicists now agree that light is somehow both a wave and a particle. Although it seems impossible to understand how anything can be both, physicists do have a number of equations for describing these things that contain both wavelength (a wave property) and momentum (a particle property). This seeming impossibility is referred to as the wave-particle duality.

Motors and Dynamos

How many electric motors are there in the room with you right now? There is at least one in your computer for starters, for the cooling fan. If you're sitting in a bedroom, you'll find motors in hairdryers and many toys; in the kitchen, motors are in just about every appliance from washing machines and dishwashers to coffee grinders and microwaves. They can also be found turning the propellers of aeroplanes and boats. Motors are one of the most useful inventions of all time…but how do they work?

Electricity, magnetism and movement

The basic idea of an electric motor is really simple: you put electricity into it at one end, and an axle (metal rod) rotates at the other end, giving you the power to drive a machine of some kind. So exactly how do you convert electricity into movement?

Suppose you take a length of ordinary wire, make it into a big loop, and lay it between the poles of a powerful, permanent horseshoe magnet. Now if you connect the two ends of the wire to a battery, the wire will jump up briefly. It's amazing when you see this for the first time. But there's a perfectly scientific explanation. When an electric current travels along a wire, it creates a magnetic field all around it. If you place the wire near a permanent magnet, this temporary magnetic field interacts with the permanent magnet's field. You've already seen how magnets will either attract or repel. In the same way, the temporary magnetism around the wire attracts or repels the permanent magnetism from the magnet, and that's what causes the wire to jump. With a bit of work and clever thought, this short movement was turned into a continuous circular motion, and the electric motor was born.

Producing electricity with movement

Just as you can create movement with electricity and magnets, you can use magnets and movement to create electricity. By moving a magnet in and out of a coil of wire, you can force electrons to move through the wire and generate electricity, albeit in tiny quantities. The best way to generate electricity is to spin a coil of wire inside a giant fixed magnet. A simple example of this is a bicycle dynamo fixed to a tyre. As the bike moves, the tyre turns a coil of wire inside a magnet and creates enough electricity to run the bike's lights.

Dynamooooo!

Elastics, Plastics and Springs

We use the concept of energy to help us describe how and why things behave the way they do. If you apply a force to an object, you may change its energy. That energy can be used to do work on the object.

Energy is called a scalar; there is no direction to energy (as opposed to vectors, which have direction). Energy is not something you can hold or touch. It is just another means of helping us to understand the world around us. Scientists measure energy in units called joules.

Season of springs

The study of springs is a whole section of physics. A spring that just sits there doesn't do much. When you push on it, you exert a force and change the arrangement of the coils. That change in the arrangement stores energy in the spring. It now contains energy and can expand and do work on other things.

Anything that is elastic (i.e. can change its arrangement and then restore itself), such as a rubber band, can store energy in the same way. A rubber band can be stretched and then it is ready to do something. That stretching involves work and increases the potential energy. You can flatten a solid rubber ball and it will want to bounce back up.

Plastic items don't store energy; they can't change their arrangement and if too much energy is put in them they will deform and break. Think about the handles of a plastic shopping bag that has been overfilled. They will deform and get longer, and if you are really unlucky they will break!

Gases storing energy

Gases are great because they can compress and expand. They act as if they were elastic. If the pressure increases and compresses gas molecules, the amount of stored energy increases. It's similar but slightly different to a spring. When you need it that energy in the compressed gas can be let out to do something.

In your car, there are shock absorbers. Some have compressed gas in the cylinders rather than springs. The energy in those cylinders keeps your car from bouncing too much if you hit a pothole.

Get Physical!

The springs in mountain bikes are what make them different from road bikes; you wouldn't want to go down a bumpy woodland trail on a hard road bike that bounces on every single bump! Mountain bikes use the springs to absorb the energy and help you stay on your bike.

E=mc²

When Einstein introduced special relativity, he also introduced one of the most famous equations known today: E=mc². It's so famous that even people with no background in physics have at least heard of it and are aware of its importance in the world we live in. However, most people don't really know what the equation means.

In simple terms, the equation explains the relationship between matter and energy: essentially, energy and matter are two different forms of the same thing.

To understand what the equation means requires four steps:

1 Define what everything in the equation means.
The first step is to understand what the different parts of the equation stand for. E is the energy of an object, m is its mass and c is the speed of light in a vacuum.

2 What is energy?
You have probably heard about lots of different forms of energy, including kinetic energy, electrical energy, thermal energy and gravitational potential energy. Energy can be neither created nor destroyed, it can only change form from one type to another.

3 What is mass? Mass is the amount of matter in an object. As far as we are concerned, this mass is fixed and will not change. It's also important to know that *mass* is not *weight*. Weight is the gravitational force felt by an object, and will vary depending on the strength of gravity in the environment the object is in. For example, you will *weigh* less on the Moon than you do on Earth, even though you have the same *mass* in both places.

4 Finally, mass and energy are the same.
The equation says that mass and energy are the same thing, so if you know how much mass an object has, you can calculate how much energy it has. The equation also shows that a small mass contains a lot of energy!

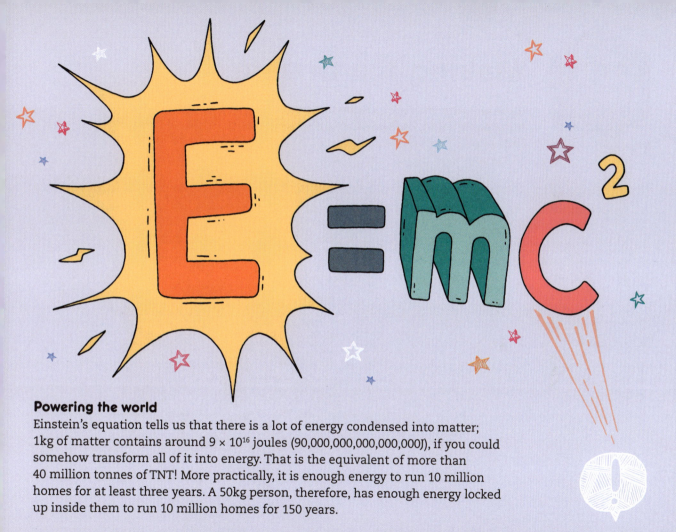

$$E = mc^2$$

Powering the world

Einstein's equation tells us that there is a lot of energy condensed into matter; 1kg of matter contains around 9×10^{16} joules (90,000,000,000,000,000J), if you could somehow transform all of it into energy. That is the equivalent of more than 40 million tonnes of TNT! More practically, it is enough energy to run 10 million homes for at least three years. A 50kg person, therefore, has enough energy locked up inside them to run 10 million homes for 150 years.

Making Ice Cream

Have you ever made ice cream at home? It's great fun and, best of all, you end up with a tasty treat!

You will need

- Measuring spoons
- 2 tablespoons of sugar
- 400ml of milk (whipping cream also works)
- Vanilla extract
- 200g salt
- Two small, sealable bags such as sandwich-size Ziploc bags
- Two very large sealable bags
- 1kg of ice cubes
- Oven mitts or a small towel
- Timer or clock

What to do

1 Before you start: In each of the small bags, place one tablespoon of sugar, 200ml of milk (or equivalent) and ¼ teaspoon of vanilla extract. Seal up each bag after adding the ingredients. Keep the bags in the refrigerator until you are ready to continue on to the procedure.

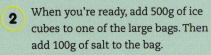

2 When you're ready, add 500g of ice cubes to one of the large bags. Then add 100g of salt to the bag.

3 Put one of the small bags you prepared into the large bag with the ice cubes. Be sure both bags are sealed.

4 Put on oven mitts or wrap the bag in a small towel, then shake the bag for at least five minutes.

5. Now add 500g of ice cubes to the other large bag, but this time do not add any salt to it.

6. Put the other small bag you prepared into this large bag. Be sure both bags are sealed.

7. Put on oven mitts or wrap the bag in a small towel and then shake the bag for at least 5 minutes, as you did before.

Mmm, I could do this experiment all day!

One of your bags should have turned into ice cream! Quick, enjoy it before it melts! Now take the bag that didn't turn into ice cream, put it into the bag with the ice and salt and mix it again for at least five minutes.

How it works

You should have seen that the ice cubes in the large bag with salt melted much more, and felt much colder, than the ice cubes in the large bag without salt. Because it was cold enough (several degrees below freezing), the bag with salt should have been able to cool the ingredients enough to harden them and turn them into ice cream, whereas the bag without salt wasn't cold enough to do this, leaving the ingredients liquid.

DO TRY THIS AT HOME

Try the experiment with different types of salt, or substitute the milk for cream or a non-dairy alternative and see what happens. Can you find the best combination?

States of Matter

We have already looked at how matter is made up of atoms, and how those atoms can be broken down into the fundamental particles. Now we are going to look at how matter behaves in the most common forms that we find it in: solids, liquids and gases.

Nnn...ice!

Solids

When the atoms inside an object are packed tightly together with a fixed shape we call that object a *solid*. You cannot walk through a solid wall. The matter is packed so tightly that it prevents you from moving through it. Solids hold their shape at room temperature.

Even in solids there is a small space between the atoms. How tightly the atoms are packed determines the density of matter. The more space there is, the less dense the material will be.

Liquids

Liquids do not hold their shape at room temperature. There is space between the atoms of a liquid and they move slightly all of the time. This allows you to stick your finger into water and pull it back out, letting the water flow back where your finger once was. But when walking through the water in the swimming pool, you have to push the water out of the way – this means that you feel the heaviness of the water. Liquids flow or pour and can take on the shape of a container. Whether liquid is poured into a wider or narrower container, the liquid will take on that new shape.

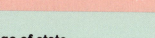

Hi! Let's let off some steam.

Gases

Gases not only do not hold their shape at room temperature, they don't even stay put! Gases are always moving. There is so much space between the atoms in gas that you can move around in them easily. When you walk from one side of the room to the other, you have walked through billions of atoms that make up the air, without really knowing that they're there. Gases will take on the shape of their container and can be compressed into a smaller space.

I'm a fluid kinda guy.

Change of state

Matter can move from one state to another, but still be the same substance. For example, an ice cube can be heated to form water and heated further to make steam, all without changing its chemical composition. Along with temperature, pressure can also change matter from one state to another. Deep in the Earth, solids turn to liquids because the heavy weight of layers and layers of the planet push down on the solids, causing them to turn to liquid magma.

H_2O

Water is the only matter on Earth that can be found naturally in all three common states of matter – solid, liquid and gas!

Get Physical!

Speed Limits

You might be able to run or swim really fast, but do you know how fast your hair grows or how quickly the Earth moves around the Sun? The list below will help you compare lots of different top speeds. Can you work out how quickly you are travelling around the Milky Way?

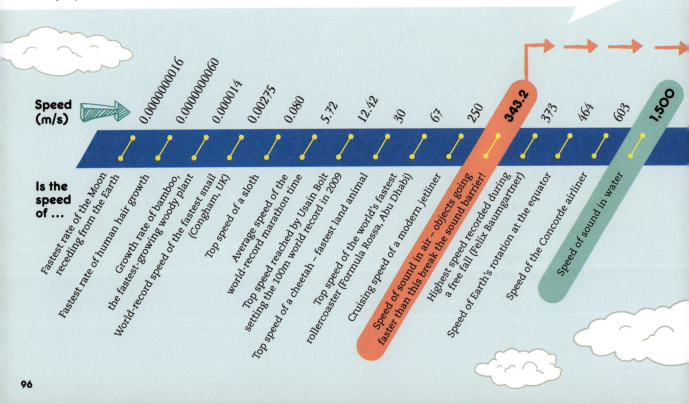

Speed (m/s)

Speed	Is the speed of...
0.000000016	Fastest rate of the Moon receding from the Earth
0.000000060	Fastest rate of human hair growth
0.000014	Growth rate of bamboo, the fastest-growing woody plant
0.00275	World-record speed of the fastest snail (Congham, UK)
0.080	Top speed of a sloth
5.72	Average speed of the world-record marathon time
12.42	Top speed reached by Usain Bolt setting the 100m world record in 2009
30	Top speed of a cheetah – fastest land animal
67	Top speed of the world's fastest rollercoaster (Formula Rossa, Abu Dhabi)
250	Cruising speed of a modern jetliner
343.2	Speed of sound in air – objects going faster than this break the sound barrier!
373	Highest speed recorded during a free fall (Felix Baumgartner)
464	Speed of Earth's rotation at the equator
603	Speed of the Concorde airliner
1,500	Speed of sound in water

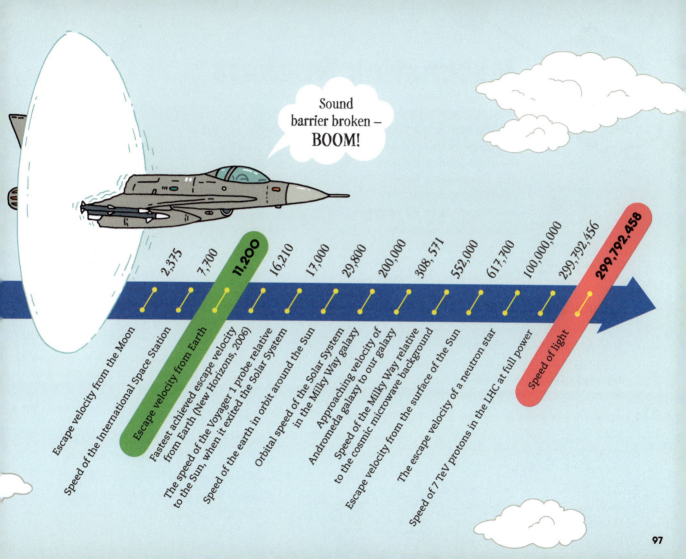

Matchstick Rockets

Making rockets that can go into space is a difficult and expensive task. Using the instructions below you can make a fully functioning rocket that can travel up to 10 metres in just a few minutes!

You will need

- Non-safety matches
- A square of tin foil approximately 5mm × 5mm
- A pin
- A large paperclip
- A tile or other heatproof surface
- A long-stem gas barbecue lighter
- Safety goggles

What to do

1. Fold the tin foil in half to make a rectangle. Fold the rectangle again lengthways and then unfold it once, leaving a rectangle with a crease running left to right down the middle.

2. Place a match with the head pointing away from you, so that the head of the match is just below the crease in the tin foil towards the left edge of the foil.

3. Place the pin on the body of the match, with the sharp end of the pin sitting over the head of the match.

4. Fold the top of the foil over the match and pin.

5. Tightly roll the tin foil around the match and pin.

6. Remove the pin and carefully place to one side. This is your matchstick rocket!

7. Bend the paperclip so that the middle section sticks up and it becomes a launch pad.

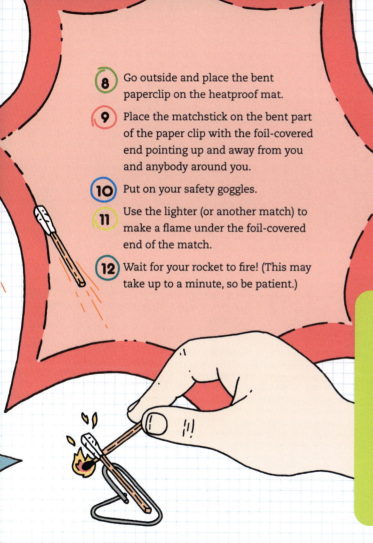

8. Go outside and place the bent paperclip on the heatproof mat.

9. Place the matchstick on the bent part of the paper clip with the foil-covered end pointing up and away from you and anybody around you.

10. Put on your safety goggles.

11. Use the lighter (or another match) to make a flame under the foil-covered end of the match.

12. Wait for your rocket to fire! (This may take up to a minute, so be patient.)

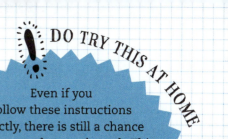

DO TRY THIS AT HOME

Even if you follow these instructions exactly, there is still a chance that your rocket won't work. This is because, while rocket science is straightforward, rocket engineering is very complex. If your rocket does fail, think about what you could do differently and try again – soon you will be building the perfect matchstick rocket!

How it works

The principle of rocket science is based around Newton's Third Law. For the rocket to be forced forwards you need an equal force working in the opposite direction, in this case, the pin that you used during the building an exhaust funnel. When the match ignited, the gases created were funnelled out along the body of the match in the opposite direction to the way you wanted the rocket to go. The smaller the exhaust the greater the force and the further the rocket will go!

Moving Sound

Have you ever stood alongside a road while an ambulance passed by with its siren on? If so, you probably noticed that as the ambulance approached, the pitch of the siren's sound (a measure of the siren's frequency) was high; and then suddenly, after the ambulance passed by, the pitch of the siren's sound was low. This is called the Doppler effect.

What is the Doppler effect?

The Doppler effect occurs for all kinds of waves: sound waves, light waves, water waves. It happens when either the source of the waves or the receiver of the waves is moving. The picture shows that the sound waves get closer together as the car moves towards you, creating a higher-pitch sound. As the car moves away, the sound waves get stretched out and you hear a lower sound.

The speed of sound is only 1,235km/h (343.2m/s), so a vehicle going at 80km/h would make a big difference in the sound that you hear! You can hear this effect if you see cars racing on TV, and it is why you should always be able to tell if a police car, ambulance or fire engine is moving towards or away from you.

But would you be able to observe the Doppler effect if you were an ambulance driver listening to your own siren?

The Doppler effect in astronomy

The Doppler effect is really useful to astronomers, who use the information about the shift in frequency of electromagnetic waves (including light) produced by moving stars in our galaxy and beyond to derive information about those stars and galaxies. We can find out lots of different things about stars by using the Doppler effect. Light emitted by stars will appear to be shifted downwards in frequency (towards the red end of the spectrum, called a *redshift*) if the star is moving away from the Earth. On the other hand, there is an upwards shift in frequency (towards the blue end of the spectrum, called a *blueshift*) of light if the star is moving towards the Earth. This technique helps astronomers find planets orbiting distant stars, work out how stars move in far-flung galaxies and even shows that most galaxies are moving away from our galaxy, the Milky Way.

Get Physical!

While the Doppler effect shows most galaxies are moving away from the Milky Way, our nearest neighbour, Andromeda, is moving towards us and is set to collide with us . . . in around 4 billion years.

Tick-tock

You may think it strange to read about clocks in a book on physics, but trying to accurately measure the passage of time has been a goal of scientists for centuries. For thousands of years, primitive devices such as water clocks, hourglasses and candles kept track of time, but the biggest breakthrough was the pendulum clock, invented in 1656, which remained the most accurate type of clock until the invention of the quartz clock in 1927 (the mechanism that powers nearly all clocks and watches today).

Side to side

The most basic and notable characteristic of a pendulum clock is given in the name, *pendulum*, which is a swinging weight that helps the clock keep time and is most commonly seen today in a grandfather clock. Galileo Galilei was the main discoverer of its wonderful property that it always takes precisely the same amount of time to complete each swing, determined by the length of the pendulum, which is the key to keeping good time! Depending on how long the pendulum is, the time it takes to swing can change, so different clocks will measure the time in different ways. Some will swing every second; others can take a whole minute just to swing back and forth once!

Get Physical!

Today the most accurate clocks are atomic clocks; they can keep time accurately to one second per 1,000 years!

Check out my kinetic-tock!

What's so good about the pendulum clock?

A pendulum does its job by converting the energy it generates from gravitational potential to kinetic. As the pendulum swings and reaches its highest point, the stored energy is at its maximum, then as it falls back towards the midpoint/lowest point the energy is then converted into kinetic energy; this is repeated as the pendulum swings from side to side. The kinetic energy is the part that keeps a clock running. The friction met by the pendulum means that as the swinging motion slows, the distance decreases over time, but it will always take the exact same amount of time to complete a swing. This creates isochronism, which essentially means 'equal amounts of time', and is the reason why pendulum clocks are so accurate.

Over time, as the pendulum's swinging slows, a clock will need to be wound to grant it the energy it needs to do its job. A heavier bob (weight) will be able to store more energy than a lighter one, therefore needing to be wound less often.

Uniting the World

The Standard Model answers many questions about the structure of matter, what it is made of and how forces affect it. However, the Standard Model is not complete, and there are several questions about the Universe that our current models just can't answer.

The main issue with the Standard Model is that it can't explain *why* particles exist as they do. It's not that physicists think the Standard Model is wrong, rather they think that it's not the full picture – there is something else that we need to discover.

Fundamental forces

There are four forces that control everything around us. They are called the fundamental forces and are:

1 The gravitational force This force is the weakest of the fundamental forces, but is still strong enough to hold galaxies together.

2 The electromagnetic force This force controls how electrons behave, and creates electric and magnetic fields.

3 The strong force This is an attractive force that binds protons and neutrons together and actually acts between quarks. It can only act over the range of the nucleus of an atom and disappears at larger distances.

4 The weak force This force is 10 million times weaker than the strong force (hence its name), but it's still stronger than the gravitational force. It acts over extremely small distances and is responsible for turning neutrons into protons.

Grand Unified Theory

One of the major goals for particle physicists is to unify the four fundamental forces into a Grand Unified Theory (GUT), a single theory that can offer a more elegant understanding of how the Universe is organised. Physicist James Maxwell took the first steps towards this goal when he combined electricity and magnetism into electromagnetism, realising that the two were both due to the movement and arrangement of electrons. Now physicists have also linked together the electromagnetic force and the weak force, as at high energies they are different aspects of the same force. This is called the electroweak force.

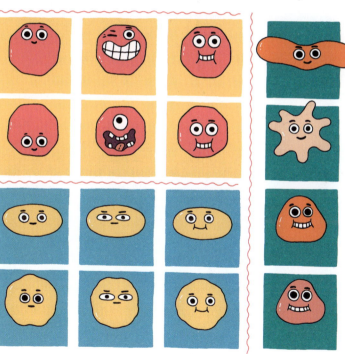

Most GUTs don't actually go as far as uniting all four fundamental forces. Instead they are trying to unite the strong force and the electroweak force, as they all have force carriers that fit into the Standard Model. For the theory to be taken further, physicists must come up with testable predictions.

Theories that work on combining all four forces also have to explain the quantum world and are called *theories of everything*, working on explaining all of fundamental physics, not just the forces. Currently no theory of everything has given an experimentally testable prediction, so this field is still completely theoretical.

Heisenberg's Uncertainty Principle

If I throw a ball to you, you can see it coming because light from the Sun (or a light bulb) bounces off the ball and into your eyes. If you did this on a very dark night you wouldn't see the ball, because no light would bounce off it and into your eyes.

But no matter how bright (or intense) the light is, the ball won't change direction when the light hits it. Every day in baseball games a form of light called radar is shot at the ball to measure its speed, and this radar never changes the speed or the direction of the ball. If it did it would be banned!

Knocking over atoms

But in the world of atoms, things are so small that light waves bouncing off atoms cause them to change direction and speed, and in some cases even knock the electrons in the atom away from the nucleus. Can you imagine being knocked over when someone shone a flashlight at you? Well, if you were as small as an atom the light would knock you head over heels!

To an atom, it's a bit like being a tennis ball moving through a room filled with bells hung on strings. When the ball collides with a bell, it rings so you know where it is. But that collision will have knocked the ball off course, meaning it's now travelling in a different direction. That ringing bell tells you where the ball was, not where it is now.

Velocity not speed

In physics you don't measure your *speed*, instead you measure your *velocity*. Velocity is your speed with a direction. For example, to give the velocity of a car travelling at 50km/h, we would say its velocity is 50km/h east (or whatever direction it was travelling in). Because of this we can't measure the velocity and

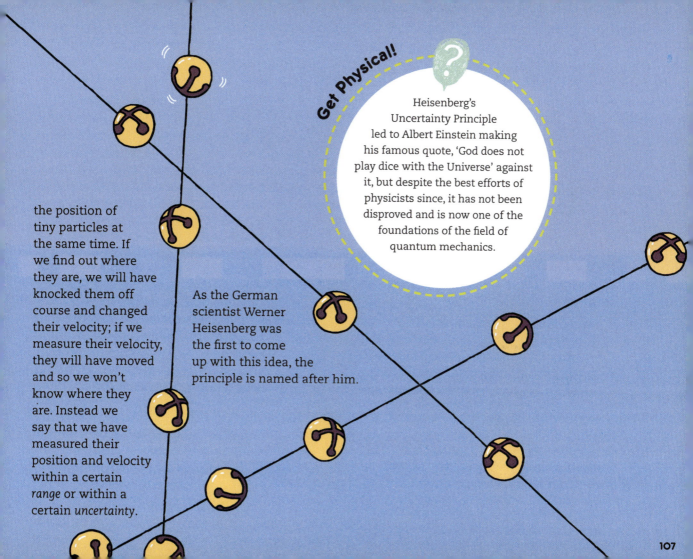

Heisenberg's Uncertainty Principle led to Albert Einstein making his famous quote, 'God does not play dice with the Universe' against it, but despite the best efforts of physicists since, it has not been disproved and is now one of the foundations of the field of quantum mechanics.

the position of tiny particles at the same time. If we find out where they are, we will have knocked them off course and changed their velocity; if we measure their velocity, they will have moved and so we won't know where they are. Instead we say that we have measured their position and velocity within a certain *range* or within a certain *uncertainty*.

As the German scientist Werner Heisenberg was the first to come up with this idea, the principle is named after him.

Brownian Motion

Brownian movement, or motion, is something that is familiar to many of us and is named after the great Scottish scientist Robert Brown. The discovery of Brownian movement was one of those accidents that happens in science, and leads to ground-breaking theories.

Brown's accidental discovery

Brown was actually a botanist, and was making his career by studying plant samples. While looking at pollen grains suspended in water under a microscope, he discovered that the pollen grains wobbled, and would gently move around the solution even though there was nothing to move them.

While not understood at the time, this motion was to lead to speculation about atoms and molecules long before they could be observed directly.

What is it?

What Brown had observed was that the pollen grains seemed to bob around through the water at random, with no way to predict their movement. This intrigued him.

He was not sure what was causing the motion, so set about ruling out various possible causes. The main achievement of Brown was proving that the movement was not due to the live pollen propelling itself, by scrutinising dead pollen grains and rock dust. He also noted that these smaller, lighter particles moved around even more than the live pollen grains!

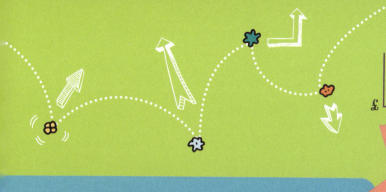

Although Brown was the first to observe and document this spectacle, he had no idea why it was actually happening. Later studies began to uncover that the Brownian movement was due to the tiny (and at the time, invisible) water molecules colliding with the pollen grains and moving them around. Despite the fact that pollen grains are 10,000 times larger than water molecules, there are so many collisions that the overall effect is strong enough to move the grains. This is what results in the jerky and unpredictable movement of the pollen grains.

While, instinctively, you would think that random movement within pollen grains would act equally in all directions and that the molecules would cancel each other out, there will actually always be a slightly stronger push one way than another.

Get Physical!

Brownian motion is one of the fundamental studies in physics, and has had far-reaching consequences in many different areas. Economists have used it to explain fluctuations in the stock market. Modern chaos theory, trying to understand the processes behind seemingly random fluctuations, also has its roots in Brownian motion.

Glossary

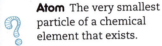

Atom The very smallest particle of a chemical element that exists.

Baryon A hadron that is formed of three quarks.

Binary system A star system that contains two stars at its centre.

Conservation of energy principle The principle that the total energy in a system remains constant no matter what changes happen in the system.

Diffraction grating A piece of glass or metal etched with parallel lines producing a spectrum through diffraction and interference of light.

Electromagnetic spectrum The distribution of electromagnetic radiation according to frequency or wavelength.

Electron spin A property of an electron (and other fundamental particles), that makes it a spinning ball of charge.

Entropy A quantity that represents the amount of energy in a system that can't be used for mechanical work, also used as a measure of disorder and randomness in the system.

Frequency The number of waves or cycles that pass a particular point each second.

Fundamental forces The four most basic forces that can act on sub-atomic particles, which currently can't be simplified into any other type of force: gravitational, electromagnetic, strong nuclear and weak nuclear.

Fundamental particle A particle that can't be broken down any more using the current understanding of particle physics.

Gluon A massless particle that transmits the strong force holding quarks together in hadrons.

Gravitational field strength or g The amount of gravitational force acting on each kilogram of matter.

Gravitational lensing The effect seen when matter (e.g. a galaxy) bends light and acts as a lens, magnifying objects behind it.

Gravitational potential energy The energy stored in an object due to its position in a gravitational field (i.e how high above the ground it is).

Graviton A theoretical particle that transmits the gravitational force that has yet to be discovered.

Hadrons A group of sub-atomic particles, including baryons and mesons, that experience the strong force.

Incident ray An incoming ray of light that strikes a surface.

Isotopes Different forms of atoms of an element that contain the same numbers of protons but different numbers of neutrons.

Kinetic energy The energy an object has when it is moving.

Leptons A sub-atomic particle that is not affected by the strong force.

Light year A unit of astronomical distance equivalent to the distance light travels in a year (about $9.5 \times 1,012$km).

Meson A hadron formed of a quark and an anti-quark.

Nanotechnology A branch of technology that operates on nanometer scales.

Neutrino A sub-atomic particle with a tiny mass and no charge that will very rarely interact with normal matter.

Nuclear fission A nuclear reaction in which a heavy nucleus splits into smaller nuclei and releases energy.

Nuclear fusion A nuclear reaction in which light nucleii fuse together to form a heavier nucleus and releases energy.

Photoelectric effect The process in which a photon hits a piece of metal and causes an electron to be emitted.

Photon A massless particle of light (or any other part of the EM spectrum) that carries energy related to its frequency.

Quantum mechanics A branch of physics that describes the behaviour of sub-atomic particles.

Quarks A group of six fundamental particles that make up heavier sub-atomic particles.

Radioactive decay The process in which the nucleus of an atom emits spontaneous radiation in the form of alpha particles, beta particles or gamma rays.

Rare earth magnets Extremely strong permanent magnets formed of rare earth elements.

Reflection The change in direction of a light ray when it hits a surface or travels through a material change.

Refraction The change in direction of a wave as it speeds up or slows down when it passes from one material to another.

Scalar A quantity that only has magnitude or size, such as mass or speed.

Standard Model A theoretical model that explains how the fundamental particles and forces work together.

Static electricity A stationary electric charge, often produced by friction, that builds up on an insulating material.

Stellar wind A continuous flow of charged particles from a star in the form of a wind.

Strong force The force that holds particles in an atomic nucleus and quarks in hadrons together.

Thermal energy or heat The internal energy of an object caused by the kinetic energy of its atoms.

Thermodynamics A branch of physics that investigates the relationship between heat and other forms of energy.

Time dilation The apparent slowing of time of a moving clock as it approaches the speed of light, as seen by a stationary observer.

Vector A quantity that has a magnitude or size and a direction, such as velocity or acceleration.

Wavelength The distance between the peak of one wave and the peak of the next one.

Wave-particle duality When something exhibits properties that are associated with both being a wave and being a particle.

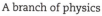

'Physics is the ultimate intellectual adventure, the quest to understand the deepest mysteries of our Universe.'

Max Tegmark